Olive,

Thank you for your love & support!

Love always!

Sue

METAMORPHOSIS

One Woman's Journey to Find Serenity & Empowerment

SUE RELIHAN

BALBOA.
PRESS

A DIVISION OF HAY HOUSE

Balboa Press books may be ordered through booksellers or by contacting:

Balboa Press
A Division of Hay House
1663 Liberty Drive
Bloomington, IN 47403
www.balboapress.com
1 (877) 407-4847

Print information available on the last page.

ISBN: 978-1-5043-4891-1 (sc)
ISBN: 978-1-5043-4893-5 (hc)
ISBN: 978-1-5043-4892-8 (e)

Library of Congress Control Number: 2016900181

Balboa Press rev. date: 03/16/2016

September 1, 2009

The Day I Decided to Change My Life

Weighing over three hundred fifty pounds, I had been attempting to hide for years. The more I tried to disappear—the more I ignored my body—the bigger I got.

But I could no longer ignore how frequently I struggled to breathe.

I was headed to Sedona, the stress of work was weighing me down. Some little voice inside my head told me I'd better go to the doctor first. I thought I just had a severe case of bronchitis and needed an antibiotic and maybe an asthma inhaler to clear my lungs. Luckily, the doctor had an opening that day.

During the intake exam, the nurse discovered that my pulse oximetry was twelve points lower than normal. Twelve points! She immediately attached me to a portable oxygen tank. My blood pressure was extremely high as well, prompting the nurse to call the doctor into the exam room ahead of other waiting patients.

He placed the bitterly cold stethoscope on my chest and listened to my heart. "I'd like you to go across the hall and get a chest X-ray. Please come straight back to this room when you're done."

Fully dressed and back in the exam room, I waited for the doctor to return.

"Your heart looks enlarged, but we can't get the whole picture from this X-ray. You need more tests. I've already called the hospital. We can send you by ambulance, or you can promise to drive directly to the emergency room. They're expecting you, either way."

I decided to drive myself. I was starving, and I wanted to stop at a drive-thru first. When I got to the emergency room, the orderlies were waiting for me with a wheelchair. I hadn't even sat down completely before they whisked me back to one of the curtained rooms. Within a matter of minutes, I was on a gurney, hooked up to all kinds of machines, including an EKG and blood pressure/heart rate monitor.

The cardiologist on call introduced himself. While he examined me, he asked, "If your heart stops, do I have your permission to restart it?"

I wasn't sure if I wanted him to....

CHAPTER 1

—— ✏ ——

My invisibility began in vitro. In a perfect world I would have been my parents' third daughter, but a few years before my birth, my mother had experienced a stillborn delivery after a car accident. It happened during the third trimester of her pregnancy. A drunk driver hit her and killed both the baby and my mother's soul.

Later, when she found out she was pregnant with me, my mother was no longer able to form a close emotional bond to her pregnancy. She was still in the throes of the trauma from that accident.

My mom never completely recovered emotionally. Home movies show me, at nine months old, fussing and crying, and my mom passing me off to my twelve-year-old sister to be comforted.

I don't have many childhood memories of being nurtured by my mother. The agony of the miscarriage had broken her spirit.

My dad was dedicated to providing for our family, but was at times a workaholic. By the time I was five, he had been promoted to the rank of captain with the Colorado State Patrol. I was proud of him. Every week I watched as he polished his badge and shined his uniform gear. He taught me a somewhat fearful respect for the firearms he carried. No matter what happened, I knew he would keep me safe, albeit from an emotional distance.

I was a very active and energetic young child. It was always a joy for me to play outside. A lunchtime game of tetherball was a lot more fun than sitting and eating my sack lunch. I loved running around the bases when we played softball during gym; even though I wasn't always very fast, it was the wind on my face that made feel alive.

Yet, I so wanted more nurturing. I turned to members of my mother's immediate family. My favorite was my doting Aunt Irene. She was both my source of fun and of comfort. She would take me to the park and push me on the merry-go-round and let me swing high into the sky. I remember how one day she painstakingly removed cactus needles from my backside when I accidently fell into the neighbor's flower garden. She was my rock until I was eight, when she died suddenly from a blood clot to her heart. If my mother had been disconnected before, there was barely a thread tying her to motherhood after her sister's death.

My own sister went off to college the same year. Suddenly my emotional support fell back to my mom, but she struggled to handle my energy. She just didn't have the emotional capacity to be fully present.

As a result, I found my solace in food. The next few years I openly used sugary food as a substitute for love. It became a substitute for the hugs and affection I longed for from my parents. It also gave me a lot of energy, but being too active was not acceptable in our household. I knew in my heart I needed to tone down my energy.

When I turned ten, my mom took me to the doctor for a physical because I was already starting puberty. I remember the doctor's cold eyes as he examined me to see if I was about to start my period. I'll never forget the tone of judgement in his deep voice when he said, "Yeah, you'd better stock up on some feminine hygiene products."

At the same appointment he also determined I weighed more than I should have at my age. He and my mom decided I needed to get a handle on my weight before it got too out of control. He sent me home with a prescription for an amphetamine diet pill and a special 800-calorie-a-day diet designed for kids. The next few months were pure hell. Even with the high-potency diet pills, I was constantly hungry. My hormones were changing and I was missing the nurturing I received from food.

While my mom couldn't connect with me emotionally, somehow, amidst the insanity, we connected when she tried to control the size of my body. She was hell-bent on keeping me from living life as a "fat girl."

"No one likes a fat girl as much as they like a thin girl," she said one day as we were headed to the doctor's office. It was her warped incentive to keep me compliant on my diet.

It wasn't long before dieting turned into a game between my mom and me. She would take me to the doctor every two weeks to be weighed. If I had lost weight, she'd reward me with a trip to Dairy Queen. Within a couple of months I learned how to manipulate the results; by putting my finger on the side table next to the scale, I'd make it look like I weighed just a pound or two less, so I could have my reward.

I couldn't outwardly get the love I longed for, and I couldn't eat what I desired. So, instead I began to master the art of invisibility while sneaking cookies.

In the corner of our kitchen, there was a large ceramic cookie jar full of my favorite forbidden treats. Supposedly it was kept stocked for my dad. Over the next few years, I learned to walk into the kitchen in full view of my parents, sneak over to the cookie jar, open and close the ceramic lid, and saunter away with a handful of cookies. Neither of my parents noticed.

I was taught at an early age how to mask my feelings, to be quiet and pretend that everything was all right, when in reality I was living with a deep sense of pain and loss. These feelings eventually turned to shame because I could never get my weight down to a size that pleased my mother. My mask covered the pain and shame that followed me through my lonely existence in high school and college.

CHAPTER 2

—— ✑ ——

After college, I tried to find a job that put my psychology degree to good use. After several months of being turned away from human-interest jobs, I was frustrated and somewhat desperate to find employment. One day my dad came home and said there was a temporary position available where he worked.

He'd retired from the State Patrol a couple of years prior and taken a position with the Arapahoe County Sheriff's Office. He was their first Work Release Coordinator. We used to joke that he spent thirty-two years putting people in jail, and suddenly it was his job to help them get out. That particular day he'd been talking to the undersheriff and found out there was a temporary position available in the Records Section. The job was mine if I wanted it, and he thought I should take it.

Believing it was just temporary, I agreed. I literally walked in the back door the next day, still invisible, bypassing all the traditional hiring practices.

About a week later one of the big burly bosses came to the Records window, leaned in, and informed me he had just made me a full-time permanent employee.

"You're welcome," was the only comment he made as he walked off.

I asked my supervisor what had happened, and she merely shrugged and said, "You know as much as I do. Let me try to find out".

She came back a little while later and told me it was merely a paperwork formality, and the only difference was I would be able to get benefits in thirty days. Otherwise everything was the same.

I was completely confused, and asked my dad about it later. He told me not to worry—it would all work out in the end. He was right, when the Records assignment was over, I moved on and spent two years doing special projects for the administration.

I've always felt grateful to Sheriff Pat Sullivan for hiring me, literally, sight unseen. Throughout the '80s and '90s, Sullivan was an enormously popular presence in the Denver area. During the early years I worked for him, both he and our agency had outstanding reputations. To that end, he had received the Sheriff of Year Award from the National Sheriff's Association.

In 1986, at an annual National Sheriffs' Association meeting, Sullivan was introduced to a new program that was designed to standardize law enforcement on a national level. Accreditation is better known in schools and hospitals, but the concept is relatively the same for public safety. The Commission on Accreditation for Law Enforcement Agencies (CALEA) establishes public safety performance standards.

Sheriff Sullivan decided during that convention he

wanted to become the first Sheriff's Office in the State of Colorado to become accredited.

I remember the day he called the undersheriff and me in to see him. I was shaking, and my voice was cracking as I sat down in his office. I was sure I was in deep trouble, but I couldn't for the life of me figure out why. Instead of yelling at me, he handed me the CALEA standards manual and the CALEA application.

"Let me know what it's going to take to get this done, and how soon you can do it." I was so relieved I wasn't in trouble that I didn't bother to ask any pertinent questions.

Right after the meeting I sat down outside his office at the typewriter and filled out the application. On the bottom of the first page there was a blank for an "Accreditation Manager." I asked the Sheriff who he wanted me to put down as the manager, and his response was, "Just put your name there for now."

Unbeknownst to either one of us, he had inadvertently made me the first female, civilian (non-cop) Accreditation Manager in the country. Neither one of us had any idea the significance of putting my name down on that page.

Fortunately I'm a fast learner, because my first task was to read and understand over 900 standards and determine how many of them were covered in our agency policy manual at the time. It took about a month for us to discover that a new Policy Manual would need to be created in order to achieve compliance with the standards.

The undersheriff decided the best way to write a new policy manual was to create a working group of people from each of the different agency functions. He attended many of the meetings, but in his absence he put me in charge of the group.

Most of the members of the group were not happy being led by a twenty-five-year-old civilian female who had never had a minute of actual law enforcement experience.

On the best days, I was slightly more than tolerated at these meetings. I credit our success to my over-achieving and people-pleasing tendencies. My bosses were thrilled with my over performance, but I seldom felt accepted. For years, I strove to fit my very round self, into their very square box. I always felt like an outsider. One of my best coping mechanisms was my ability to shut down and mask my hurt feelings, using the skill of invisibility I'd refined in my childhood.

Just like in childhood, I believed if I tried just a little bit harder, worked just a little bit longer, or even lost a bunch of weight, eventually I would be accepted.

Our agency received initial accreditation in July of 1988. I felt so proud of this enormous accomplishment, but I still didn't feel like I had been seen or accepted at work.

Typically after an agency was initially accredited, a sworn Accreditation Manager was promoted or moved to another assignment. Many times the agency lost the consistency to stay accredited. In time, CEOs realized that hiring civilian managers kept that from happening. Over the next couple of years Sheriff Sullivan acquired the reputation of being a visionary when he started the trend of appointing a civilian Accreditation Manager. Over the years when I heard the topic discussed, I laughed to myself but chose to keep my mouth shut. My ego didn't like admitting that my selection really was just a fluke.

In 1991, a group of local Accreditation Managers started the Rocky Mountain Accreditation Network (RMAN) as a resource and support for agencies participating in the CALEA process. All of the other managers in the region were mid-ranking sworn officers; I was the only civilian. By that time I had developed a reputation as someone other agencies could count on to help them get accredited. Sheriff Sullivan was usually willing to lend me to other agencies for a week at a time to help guide them in policy development and/or compiling compliance. Because of my success rate no one openly questioned my gender or my non-sworn status. My mask of confidence, albeit fake, was firmly in place.

The day we decided to establish the formal RMAN group was another pivotal day in my life. I had just left the lunch meeting in which the group was officially organized and was driving back across town when I felt ill. There was tightness in my chest, and my heart raced. Instead of going back to the office, I detoured to the closest emergency room, convinced I was having a heart attack.

As it turned out it was just a panic attack, but it was my body's attempt to send me a message. Unfortunately, it was a message that would take me many more years to decipher. Instead of listening to the signal from my body, I ignored it, donned my invisibility cloak, and took a deep dive into the world that never really fit for me.

I let go of my heart's desire, which was to step into the world of the healing arts, and shut myself off from both my spirit and my physical body. I turned the "Closed" sign on my heart and began to live solely in my head. I spent years building my law-enforcement reputation, and prided myself on how well I could hide from the world in plain sight.

Because of my success as an Accreditation Manager, I was appointed as a paid part-time Assessor (consultant) for CALEA, giving me the opportunity to go around the country and inspect other law-enforcement agencies. As a CALEA Assessor, it became customary for me to team up with law-enforcement executives to determine how well another agency was being managed based on established national standards. It was a fabulous opportunity to see how the "best of the best" performed their law-enforcement responsibilities.

During this same time, I became one of a few dozen national experts regarding law-enforcement standards and had the chance to be on the task force that created the third edition of the CALEA standards manual.

It was a remarkable time in my life. No one realized I was still wearing my cloak of invisibility.

For several years during a variety of life experiences, I excelled at putting on a mask, pretending everything was all right, and making my job the primary focus of my life.

CHAPTER 3

— ✒ —

In 2002 I had just finished an out-of-state CALEA assessment and came home to a message that my dad had the flu. He had fallen in 2000 and had spent eighteen months in a rehab/assisted living center as he rebuilt his strength and regained enough independence to move back to the house where I had grown up.

He had hated losing his self-sufficiency and living in that little one-room apartment. He'd only agreed to stay there if we hired a private physical therapist to help him work to rebuild his strength rapidly. He was very determined and proud to get stronger again. It took almost two years, but eventually he succeeded and moved home.

Later on that fateful Saturday night, he called me to tell me he'd gotten up to go to the bathroom but fell along the way, and he wanted me to come over and help him get back into bed. My dad was a very big man, 6'3" and 275 pounds, so I knew I couldn't get him back in bed by myself. I suggested we call the fire department so they could help me lift him. He wasn't happy with the idea but agreed that I was going to need the help. I called them as I headed out the door. I was scared and probably broke a few traffic laws as I drove to my dad's house, yet I was surprised when I'd managed to beat the fire department there, despite my house being twice as far as their fire station. Guess I'd had a bit of a lead foot.

The minute I walked in, my dad asked me to try to get him back up into bed. I could tell he was much weaker than he had been before I'd left town. Thankfully, the firefighters were right behind me and offered their help. Since Dad had been in law enforcement for forty years, most of which with the State Patrol covering auto accidents, a few of the older firefighters remembered him.

They touched my heart deeply in the way they treated him with respect and care.

Dad was very weak. It took four guys to lift him back into his bed. When they checked his vitals, he and I were both surprised at how low his pulse was (below 60) while his blood pressure was actually elevated. They told us he appeared to be dehydrated, and it would be a good idea to take him to the emergency room and have him checked out.

Dad wasn't thrilled about going to the hospital, but he was too weak to put up much of a fight. They talked with him for a few minutes, and the paramedic team somehow convinced him he was doing them a favor by letting them take him in to get checked out. I will be forever grateful to the guys who responded to his house that night because they knew exactly how to treat my dad. As they loaded him in the ambulance I could hear him telling them about how he'd counted on guys like them when he investigated traffic accidents during his days with the State Patrol. Dad always knew how to connect with other people.

Instead of riding in the ambulance, I followed them in my car. We were at the hospital for a couple of hours when the attending doctors realized my dad might have more going on than just the flu and admitted him.

Later that morning, after my sister came to the hospital, I went home to get some sleep. It had been a long night, plus I was still tired from my trip. Despite my exhaustion, though, I was too stressed to fall asleep and couldn't get the much-needed rest I should have. I just lay in my bed, staring at the ceiling, running through all of the events that had happened.

As I tossed and turned, I couldn't quite shake the feeling of dread that enveloped me. Finally, I drifted off into a few hours of restless sleep.

CHAPTER 4

— ✒ —

The next two weeks went by in a blur. Within a couple of days of being admitted to the hospital, the doctors determined my dad had an impacted colon. Sadly, the tests they had run to determine what was wrong with him ended up aggravating the impaction. At first the doctors wanted to do surgery, but they decided to wait a couple of days to see if his condition improved.

While waiting for him to rebuild his strength in order to have surgery, he and I had a lot of time to talk. The bond between us grew stronger. We spent hours just reminiscing. He repeatedly told me how proud he was of me. It was one of the first times I ever remember us talking about my choice of working in law enforcement. He gave me advice on how to handle the new sheriff who had recently been appointed as CEO for my agency. My dad was a major Pat Sullivan fan and was a little concerned about the politics of the new incoming sheriff. Little did we know how prophetic his words would end up being.

My dad had retired from our agency before this new sheriff started, but he remembered him because they had worked together years earlier when my dad had been a State Trooper.

Dad told me to be careful and to make sure I stayed on the right side of the political fence in order to stay in the good graces of the new administration. He reminded me about how he had failed to align with the right side of a political battle years prior in his career with the Colorado State Patrol. He had paid a heavy price as a result. I assured him I knew what I was doing. I never dreamt I would be anywhere other than on the right side of the new administration.

During his hospital stay, we also talked about when I was fifteen, and he wanted my help to dig a well in our backyard to put in an outdoor pump for his garden. It was in the late 70s and Denver was in a drought condition. He wanted to be able to water his tomato plants, so he made me a deal that if I helped him dig the well, he would buy me my first car. It had taken us several weekends of hard labor—blood, sweat, and my tears at least—before we finished digging a 22-foot deep cistern-type well. Once it was done, I loved watching him attach the old hand pump from the farm in Kansas where he had grown up. I think we were all shocked the first time he hooked the pump up and water actually came out of it. Granted, it would only supply enough water to fill two five-gallon buckets at a time, but he was so happy. It was one of my first great accomplishments, and I had a lingering, deep sense of self-satisfaction over our new well.

I admitted to him that back then I had wanted him to buy me a brand-new Chevy Camaro, and, to this day, I still felt as if I worked hard enough that summer to earn one. We laughed because instead of a Camaro, he'd gotten me a used Ford Maverick. Nonetheless, I finally had my very own first car. I remember the fabulous sense of freedom that I enjoyed that summer in my Maverick. While we were laughing, I jokingly said, "Yeah, but it wasn't a Camaro."

He looked at me and said, "Why don't you go buy yourself one now? I know you can afford it."

"Dad, when you get out of the hospital, you and I can go shopping, and you can help me pick it out." I reached over and rearranged the oxygen nubs in his nose.

He laughed, "And maybe I will buy myself a new Cadillac while we're at it." His eyes took on a serious gaze. "I'm proud I was able to raise you to be financially responsible." He smiled gently and took my hand. "I know, if something happens to me, that you and your sister will never be as poor as I was."

His upbringing during the Great Depression had left a deep impact on him, and he had determined he would never be poor again. I got tears in my eyes. "Daddy, I'd rather you live long enough to spend all your money."

I will never forget this incredibly tender moment between my dad and me because it was the last time he and I had any time alone.

The next day, he and his doctor determined he probably was not going to be a candidate for surgery. At that moment, the finality of their decision didn't quite hit me. He was very calm and told my sister and me that he was opting for palliative care and, with our agreement, he would sign the papers to transfer to a hospice facility.

The doctors told us he could live several more weeks or even months, but this way they could do whatever was necessary to keep him comfortable. Part of me understood his unwillingness to have another surgery, but another part of me wanted him to fight. I knew I wasn't ready to lose my daddy.

The next day they moved him to the hospice center not far from my office. After my sister and I had helped him get settled in, I went to the Sheriff's Office to work for a couple of hours. I hadn't been in the office very much in the last couple of weeks and needed to escape to the one place where I felt as if I were still in control.

That night when I left the office, I drove through Arby's and got dinner for us. The hospice folks had told us my dad could have anything he wanted, and he said he wanted an Arby's sandwich and a strawberry milkshake.

When I got to the hospice, Dad was in a great mood. My sister was already there, and they were watching the news. I could tell that he was doing okay. They finally managed to control his pain with morphine, and he looked just a little tipsy. Dad had never been a heavy drinker, so it was a relief to see his eyes shining and him feeling no pain.

The three of us sat and talked and laughed for a couple of hours. He told us some of his favorite stories, and we truly had an enjoyable evening, considering the circumstances. At about 9:30, my sister and I decided to leave for the night. As we were walking out, we stopped in the hallway outside his room and discussed the logistics of the next few days. Primarily, we wanted one of us to be with him most of the time and were deciding the best way to split the days. The doctors told us he could be in hospice up to six weeks, and we needed to coordinate our schedules.

As we were standing outside his room talking, Dad called out to us to tell us one more story. It was his favorite story about an old Colorado State Patrol Chief that we heard dozens of times throughout our lives.

My first reaction was to say, "Oh Dad, we know." Thankfully something stopped me.

My sister and I stood in his room while he told us the story that in the end made him laugh with complete abandon. He had a gleam in his eyes that spoke volumes of how happy he was at that moment.

We all said our good nights one more time. I left the hospice facility feeling content from our evening together.

I went home and fell right to sleep knowing that my dad was satisfied with his decision, and that all was well for the night, but around 3:30am, my phone rang.

It was my sister saying the hospice nurse had just called. Dad had taken a sudden turn for the worse, and we should head over right away if we wanted to be with him when he died. She drove by to pick me up, and we went back to hospice. Sure enough, when we got to his room he was unconscious and a nurse's aid was sitting with him. She uncovered his legs and showed us they were mottling from a lack of blood flow. She also pointed out that his breathing was labored. She explained both of these were signs of impending death and he would likely be gone in just a matter of hours.

I think the change in his condition happened so quickly that neither one of us knew what to do besides tell him we loved him and hold his hand. We talked to him and gave him encouragement to let go as he took his last breaths. Those last hours were some of the longest and saddest of my life.

When his breathing stopped and he left us for good, I was so far removed from my heart I could not cry right away. Instead, I went into autopilot and began making arrangements for his funeral. My stress skyrocketed because I was physically exhausted from lack of sleep, and I was emotionally drained from losing the most important person in my life. My doctor prescribed an anti-depressant, and when I took it I was even less emotionally present. The days around his death and burial are still very fuzzy to me.

I do remember how packed the chapel was on the day of his funeral. It was standing room only with over 300 people in attendance. The State Patrol and the Sheriff's Office Honor Guards led the lights-and-siren processional from the chapel to the graveside. Dad would have been very pleased that so many of his fellow Masons and his law-enforcement brothers and sisters were there to honor him. It was a full-honor burial with "Taps" and a 21-gun salute. As soon as they folded and gave the flag to my sister, a strong breeze blew through the cemetery and every hair on my body stood up. It was at that moment deep inside my heart, I knew my dad was truly gone.

I wish that I had better recall of all the people who came to the service or by the house afterward, but sadly, that conscious memory is lost to me. All I knew was I had a gaping hole in my life, with no idea how I was going to fill it.

CHAPTER 5

— ♪ —

Five months after my dad died, I still felt as if my world had been tossed upside down. I needed a diversion from the stress of settling my dad's estate, and work wasn't cutting it. Standing and facing uncomfortable feelings wasn't my strong suit. I preferred to push my stress aside and ignore it completely. I felt as if I needed a distraction.

One night at dinner a dear friend suggested I try online dating again and told me about a new site that was dedicated to large people.

What the heck? I thought. *It's worth a try.* I figured it would give me something else to focus on besides the void my father's death had left in my world. Little did I know, I'd drag my unresolved vulnerability and invisibility along with me.

I remember the exact day I received a "wink" from someone named Big Mike. When I checked out his profile, one of the first things that attracted my attention was that he worked in the security field. I wasn't exactly sure what that meant, but I had high hopes he wouldn't be intimidated by my law enforcement career, and we might have some things in common.

I decided to respond to him. I liked his profile, and I could feel just a glimmer of hope rising. I was tempted to sit in front of my computer and wait for his response, yet I knew that was the mark of an overly desperate woman. Instead, I headed out to a memorial luncheon for the sister of a dear friend who'd been in a horrible car accident.

All throughout lunch, I couldn't wait to get home to see if I had a response to my message. It was uncanny but I had a strong sense that Big Mike was someone special.

I was thrilled when I saw he had answered me. I was even happier when I saw not only had he answered my wink, but also attached his picture. When I opened it, I saw one of the most handsome, tall, large men I'd ever seen. My heart skipped a beat. Boy, was he good looking!

I was a little unsure of how to react to him wearing a very colorful Native American Indian outfit. The picture also showed a large group of other colorfully dressed Indians. His profile had said he was Native American, but I had skimmed right past that detail. He explained that he had recently been to the Denver March Powwow, and the picture he sent was taken by a friend of his at that event. I remember just shaking my head when he said he hoped I didn't find him too ugly and asked for me to send him a picture of myself in return.

I took a deep breath. Did I have the courage to send him a current picture and let him see how fat I really was? I knew this particular website was marketed specifically for large people, but I couldn't stop myself from wondering what he'd think.

Oh, what the hell, I'll just send one and see what happens! Nothing ventured, nothing gained. I hit the enter key.

I sat in front of the computer barely able to breathe, truly hoping he was right there at his computer and would answer right away. Fear was like a scared rabbit in my chest. Luckily, it didn't take too long, and his reply sent a wave of relief through my body.

"You are beautiful."

Although I didn't believe him, it was so nice for someone to say the words I'd waited a long time to hear again. At that moment, my heart slowly began to open.

"Thanks," was my quick reply because I couldn't figure out what else to say, and I found myself a little shy. As I hit the send key, I said a quick prayer: *Please let this be the man of my dreams.*

That was on a Friday. I woke up the next morning wondering if I would hear from him. We hadn't exchanged enough information for me to know what to expect. I was still a little leery of dating, and although he looked good on paper, I had a lot of skepticism based on my previous relationships. I knew there were many frogs in the online dating pond. I sincerely doubted there were very many decent men who wanted to make love with a woman who had a body as large as mine. If I couldn't accept the size of my body, how could I ever expect someone else to love it?

I was excited when there was a message from him including his private email address. One of the first characteristics I noticed was that he was up early. He sent the email at 5:30 in the morning. I was also happy because he was on AOL, which meant I could do a little cyber stalking. I wanted to look at his online profile and make sure everything matched up before I sent him my personal information. I was eager, but I kept telling myself to move slowly and stay a little bit cautious.

At first glance, his AOL profile lined up pretty closely with his dating profile, and I had the bonus of viewing a few more pictures of him. I checked his physical stats on his profile and saw he listed himself at 6'4" and 325 pounds. I just kept thinking he was such a good-looking, very large man. It didn't take long for me to decide to send him an email so he would have my AOL address.

One of the biggest advantages to AOL at that time was the ability to add him to my Buddy List and chat on Instant Messaging. It was much easier to IM than to send messages through the dating site.

When I asked Michael what he did for a living, he told me he was in charge of security for a large corporation. He said he was responsible for supervising the other security guards and, as a team, they provided 24-hour-a-day security. I wanted to confirm he was really in the security field before I shared too much about myself. I sat and pondered how to go about this while I waited for his response to my latest email.

He replied to my email right away with an AOL "friend" invitation, and I happily accepted it. I loved that I could see whether or not he was online. Most of the time, I kept my status as *invisible*, but once he sent me a friend request I changed my status to *available*. I felt very available.

Almost immediately, I received an invitation to start an

Instant Message. We spent most of the morning chatting. I no longer remember all of the details of what we talked about that first day, but what I do remember was that he shared enough about himself that I began to believe he was real.

He told me he'd worked for the same security company for years and gave me enough details that it helped me to realize he might just be authentic, and I began to relax just a little bit. One of the first things I was attracted to was his great sense of humor, and that he paid me a lot of compliments. I sat on my couch for hours with my laptop, totally tuned into our conversation on AOL. I was so happy to have someone pay attention to me in a romantic way. It had only been a day, and I was already beginning to feel that fabulous twitterpated new love feeling.

We spent the weekend exchanging emails and instant messages. I don't think I slept much at all that weekend. Between chatting—and thinking about chatting—I didn't get anything else accomplished. For the first time in several months, I felt happy. I was amazed at what I had learned about him so far. He had just turned fifty the previous week, which meant he was eight years older than I was. It didn't take long to determine he was a liberal and was very involved with some local Native American activist groups.

He told me a little bit about his family history as well. He was raised by his paternal aunt and had very little contact with his biological parents. He and his aunt were very poor when he grew up near an Indian Reservation in Oklahoma, but he never said a negative thing about any of his relatives. He explained he didn't have any full-blood siblings, but he did have a couple of half-brothers with whom he said he wasn't very close. He also told me he had a number of "taken" brothers and sisters. It was the first time I'd heard that concept, and it fascinated me. His closest relative was his "taken" brother Lance. He explained that similar to a "blood brother" pact, Native Americans not related by birth frequently take on siblings by swearing deep loyalty to each other. Except for not sharing blood, I understood Lance was Michael's brother in every way possible.

As I went to sleep that night, I found myself amused because, apparently, I'd learned some decent interrogation skills while hanging around all those cops. I managed to ferret out quite a bit of information about a man I'd only known for three days.

One of my better defense mechanisms was spending a lot of time chatting, but not revealing a lot about myself. I did notice he hadn't spent much time asking me about myself. He did ask about where I worked, and I told him. I just shook my head when he assumed I was a dispatcher at the Sheriff's Office. At that point, I decided not to correct him. I wasn't sure how he'd feel if he knew I held more of an executive position, and that I likely made twice as much money as he did. The concept didn't bother me, but I didn't know how his ego would respond. Whether or not our financial differences would bruise his ego was a worry for another day.

I was grateful I could check email from work, although I'm a little reluctant to admit the amount of time and energy I spent those first few days exchanging messages with Michael. As it turned out, he also worked a Monday-through-Friday day job but apparently had constant email access and not a lot of other distractions. The number of emails we exchanged was beyond my wildest imagination.

Within days, I realized there didn't seem to be any topic with him that was off limits. I wondered if he was as suitable in person as he sounded in his emails. I just hoped I still felt as connected after we met face-to-face.

We set up our first date the following Friday, and I could hardly endure the wait. I treasured the amazing belly-buzzing feeling that put a smile on my face whenever I thought about some of our email exchanges. To this day, I still believe there's no better feeling in the world than those first days of being completely infatuated with someone.

With each email and each conversation, I opened my heart to the possibility of being loved. We hadn't even met, and I'd already begun to feel like Michael was the one with whom I would spend the rest of my life.

A lot of what sealed the deal was when he said he didn't care about the size of my body. He told me repeatedly that my large body meant there would just be more of me for him to love. He explained that many of the Native women are big girls and he thought they were very beautiful. He even sent me a picture of two of his nieces to prove his point. I just couldn't help but wonder if he would still say the same things after we met, and, more importantly, if I would be able to believe him.

When Friday rolled around, I was already comfortable enough with Michael to let him come pick me up at my house. Normally for all first dates, I would meet at a public location in order to have an escape route with my own transportation readily available. Somehow during the week, Michael convinced me, actually he insisted, on picking me up at the house and treating me like a lady. He told me it was very important for him to treat me right, and he could already sense I'd never had a man do that for me before. I enjoyed that he was an old-fashioned gentleman when it came to dating.

With a bit of remaining skepticism, I picked a place for dinner close enough to my house that if I needed to, I could always walk home. I left the office early that day, went home, and did all of the primping I could think of to prepare for my date. I must have pulled five or six different outfits out of the closet until I figured out exactly what I wanted to wear. The restaurant where we were going was casual, so jeans would have been appropriate, but that was not the first impression I wanted to make. Instead, I wore a casual dress and low heels.

I was grateful I had dressed up a little because he showed up at my front door in a suit jacket and tie. My first thought was that he was an absolutely gorgeous, powerful presence of a man. I loved the way he combed his jet-black hair, spiking it on the top. I looked forward to the moment when I could run my fingers through it.

When we left my house that night in his pickup truck, I felt on top of the world. Michael owned a fully-loaded Chevy, and it even had a small television inside of it. When I asked him about the TV, he said he took a lot of road trips with his brothers and they usually slept in the truck.

The TV connected him to the weather and sports when they were out camping.

When we got to Poppies, because we had not made reservations, the only seating they had available was a small booth in the front. As I look back, it must have been funny to see the two of us very large people squeeze ourselves into that small booth. Neither one of us had the courage to ask to move.

While we sat and talked over dinner, one thing I noticed right away was how the glasses he wore resembled my dad's glasses. I wasn't quite conscious of the comparison; I just knew it somehow put me at ease.

Dinner was good and I enjoyed talking with him, but that booth was terribly uncomfortable. Needless to say, we didn't linger at dinner very long. We were both relieved when the check came, and I was pleased when he didn't hesitate to pay. Luckily, there was a Dairy Queen nearby, so we walked over there for dessert.

As we drove home, he held my hand. I seriously considered asking him to come inside. Just as I was about to say something, he spoke up and said that he'd had a wonderful time and already couldn't wait to see me again.

Somehow, I knew from his tone that inviting him in would not have been the next right move. I have to admit, though, I was a little confused when he pulled into my driveway but didn't kill the engine. He told me not to move until he could come around and open my door. I think he felt amused by the stunned look on my face and told me it was about time someone treated me like a lady.

Because he left the truck running, I knew he was not

planning to stay. Instead, he walked me to my door and made sure it was unlocked. He took me in his arms and kissed me passionately. He looked deeply into my eyes and told me he respected me enough to wait. It was as if he read my mind, knowing how much I wanted him to come in and spend the night.

As we were standing there in an embrace, I was spellbound by the size of his body and how safe I felt within his arms. He wore a nice musky cologne, and I knew the scent would stay with me.

After just a few minutes of kissing, he held me at arm's length and told me he needed to leave. He had to get up early the next morning because he was going to Colorado Springs for the weekend with his brother. I wished him a great weekend and told him I'd be looking forward to talking to him when he returned.

When I walked into the house, I felt confused. I couldn't make up my mind. Should I pout because he was leaving town, or jump for joy because he was the first guy I had met in a very long time who made me feel like a lady? Instead of either option, I grabbed a beer and sat on the couch repeatedly playing the last week over in my mind. I was becoming aware that I'd be willing to walk over broken glass for this man.

CHAPTER 6

—— ✤ ——

The next week at work, people began to notice a shift in my attitude. I had a couple of people ask me what was going on in my life that made me so happy.

My direct supervisor wasn't quite as thrilled. I may have been happier, but my work was not nearly as efficient as it had been. Before I met Michael, I had been a workaholic— easily working ten to twelve hours a day, often six days a week. My life had completely revolved around my job. For many years, my position at the Sheriff's Office was my sole identity. That started to shift before my dad died, but changed even more when I met Michael. Plus the time I'd spent checking and responding to his emails didn't help my productivity, but by that point, I was too mesmerized by my infatuation to care.

Michael was in a job where he could check email constantly, which meant as soon as I would respond to him, he would immediately respond to me. There was a constant circle of emails the next week leading up to our second official date. I was floating on a cloud.

It was impossible to concentrate on writing a new policy when my every thought turned to our next encounter. I felt consumed with the idea of falling in love. Maybe this would be my chance to make up for all of my previously failed relationships; maybe it wasn't too late to have a healthy, loving relationship. On some level, I knew I was desperate for love, but on another level I truly didn't care that I felt so desperate. Compartmentalizing my feelings came naturally to me.

I couldn't help but wonder what sex was going to be like. He was such a big man—and I was a big girl— and I wasn't exactly sure how easily (or not) we would fit together. All I knew was every time the thought of Michael crossed my mind, I got that butterfly kisses feeling deep in the pit of my belly.

His first kiss was so sweet, and there was a lustful hunger that convinced me we would not get through another date without having sex. My intuition told me, because he was already so attentive to me, he would likely be an incredible lover. Although I couldn't articulate exactly why, I already felt very comfortable with him.

Together, we decided that for this second date, I would cook him dinner at my house. I asked him what type of food he liked. He assured me he would enjoy eating anything I fixed.

Little did he know, I wasn't a very good cook. I had scoured the Internet for three days looking for the perfect meal. I ended up choosing something called Mexican Meatloaf. I got off work early and went to the grocery store, making sure I had enough time to shower, get ready, and have dinner cooking.

Thank God I had stocked enough beer to have a little

liquid courage to carry me through preparing for the evening. It had been a long time since I had primped for a date I knew would end with sex. Without the extra courage, I don't know that I could have pulled it off.

Even with the extra boost, I felt nervous about the evening. It was important to me for everything to be perfect. I was still feeling the need to make up for my body size. Since perfection was rarely an option in my mind, the alcohol numbed me from the reality of the profound discomfort I felt.

I was not surprised, between Michael's military background and his work as a security guard, when he was punctual. I was, however, pleasantly surprised to see him wearing a collared shirt and sport jacket. He told me it was another sign of respect to be dressed up, even for a casual night at home.

I was also pleased that as soon as he came in the door, he took me in his arms and kissed me passionately. I had fantasized about our next kiss all week. It was hard to pull myself away, but I found my voice, invited him in, and told him to make himself at home.

Dinner was almost ready, but we made the mistake of sitting down on the couch to have a beer. We started kissing, and I ended up burning the meatloaf. I was devastated, but Michael was such a gentleman and blamed himself for distracting me. He suggested we cut off the bottom burnt part, and still eat it.

Even with the dinner disaster, the conversation between us was light and breezy. He chatted a little bit more about his life, and specifically about his weekend in Colorado

Springs with his brother and several of their other Indian friends. They had been invited to be the host Southern Drum at a powwow. He began describing some of the ins and outs of the world of powwows, and I found myself fascinated by his explanations.

I shared a couple of funny stories about the people I worked with as well. There was always something going on at my office, and he laughed as I told him about some of the shenanigans the guys at work had pulled off. I was grateful he understood the sometimes dark nature of law-enforcement humor. The burnt dinner disaster had been forgotten.

When dinner was over, we moved back to the couch. He took me in his arms, told me I was beautiful, and began to kiss me. Being in his arms was exactly what I was craving and immediately he made me feel safe and cherished. I had never dated a man that much larger than me, and I enjoyed feeling protected in his embrace. I remember thinking I was grateful I had made the extra effort to get waxed and buffed.

As we made out on the couch like a couple of teenagers, the rest of the world disappeared. My entire life became wrapped up solely in how good it felt being held in Michael's arms. I did not want that feeling to ever end. At one point he sat back, looked me in the eyes, and told me he had waited a long time to find someone as special as me. I longed to believe him because there was a look of deep sorrow in his eyes. I chose to ignore it for the moment and instead got lost in his kisses.

He moved his kisses from my mouth, and found the

place on the side of my neck that makes me melt. At that moment I was in heaven. He helped me remove my blouse and my bra and kissed my breasts, and I felt like he completely adored my body.

When he started kissing and caressing my belly, I was taken by surprise. My belly has always been the part of my body I hated the most because it's the biggest part of my body and the source of my greatest body shame. He told me how beautiful it was, and I was completely confounded, and simultaneously thrilled beyond measure, when he devoted all of his attention to my stomach.

Part of me wanted to push him away, and part of me never wanted him to stop. I knew at that moment I would move heaven and earth to please this man. When he took my hand to lead me to my bedroom, I didn't hesitate to follow.

I shifted my focus to concentrating on undressing and pleasuring him. My hands and my mouth found their way around his body. It was the first time I was free from all my inhibitions. He had found a way to cross a barrier I hadn't even realized I'd created.

We spent hours exploring each other's bodies until we were both spent and blissfully exhausted. I felt safe, tucked into the side of his body. It was the warmest, most comforting feeling I had experienced in a very long time. Within minutes, I drifted off into a peaceful, restful slumber. Even his snoring was a rhythmic melody that made my heart happy. I truly believed I'd found nirvana, and I never wanted it to end.

I don't know how long we were asleep, but before I

knew it, Michael kissed my cheek and thanked me for a beautiful night. He said he would let himself out and would call me later. When I woke up enough to figure out what was going on, I realized it was 4:30 in the morning.

I couldn't figure out why he was leaving. I had planned a leisurely Saturday morning breakfast, followed by more hours in bed, but when I told him my plans he said he had things he needed to do. I hated that he was leaving because it felt like rejection and didn't make sense to me.

As I lay in an empty bed, my mind began to whirl. Why would he possibly need to leave at 4:30 in the morning? My thoughts were wild and ran rampant. Could he be married? Had I misinterpreted the night? Was he upset with me? What could make him get up and leave in the middle of the night? The more my mind spun, the more I was convinced something must be terribly wrong. I didn't want to lose what I'd felt. I knew I couldn't possibly survive the rest of my life without feeling the way I did last night. It felt like my life depended on finding out what happened and what I needed to do to make it right.

After he had left, I was so tired that I fell back to sleep. By the time I got up again, I had an email from Michael. He explained he had gotten a 911 page with an emergency at his office. I wasn't sure whether or not I should be annoyed, because he had not clearly communicated what was going on. Instead I chose to feel relieved there wasn't something wrong between us. I decided to be grateful so that I could go back to concentrating on the good times we'd had in the last couple of weeks.

I didn't care that we didn't have another specific date

set. His email reassured me he was still very interested and wanted to be with me. It was all I needed to relax back into my feeling of infatuation and that's how I floated through the weekend.

I hate to admit how easily and quickly my magical thinking took over, but we had only been together for a couple of weeks and I was already planning my future with him. The energy between us was magical, and I could not imagine what my life would be like without feeling someone cherish me as deeply and passionately as Michael had in those first two dates.

CHAPTER 7

—— ✒ ——

The next couple of weeks seemed to fly. My relationship with Michael slowly crept into almost every aspect of my day. I still worked my regular schedule; however, much of my time and energy was either devoted to emailing Michael or thinking about the emails. Our relationship had obviously taken first place in my mind. I stopped caring as much about my job or what was going on at work. It was a good distraction.

There was a new political regime forming at my agency. Instead of focusing on the new regime, I directed all of my attention to finally having the *LOVE* I had never even allowed myself to dream about. This experience was so different for me, because at one time I would have felt consumed by the changes in my work environment, but now—*Meh!* I was more than ready for a change in my personal life, and I just didn't care as much about my job as I once had.

Michael and I emailed during the day, and instant messaged throughout the evening. Occasionally, we would talk on the phone, but we had decided early on that it was easier to communicate via written text. It seems strange to me in looking back that I didn't think it was weird that we didn't talk more on the phone. We didn't spend much time together in person either, even though he lived within two miles of my house. We both seemed content with our copious instant messages.

We did continue to enjoy a date at least once a week. For the most part we went out to dinner, and then Michael would come back to my house and we would have mind-blowing sex. Occasionally I stayed over at his apartment and he'd treat me to an early morning breakfast. He made homemade biscuits and gravy from scratch, with scrambled eggs, bacon, and fried potatoes. I was surprised by how much he enjoyed cooking, often singing and dancing while he stirred food on the stove.

After we had been dating for about eight weeks, Michael asked me during one of our conversations if I would cook him dinner again. I laughed, surprised he was willing to take the risk because of our disastrous meatloaf episode. He reassured me, saying he knew I could cook, and added that we needed to talk about something very important to him.

I'd begun to notice earlier in the week that the tone of his emails had shifted. I wondered what was going on in his world, but up until that point when I asked him about it, he said he'd just gotten busy at work.

I'm an intuitive woman, and something inside of me told me to pay attention. Michael dismissed my questions by explaining that there were major changes in his office, and he simply didn't have the same amount of time available to email me. It felt plausible to me considering the tremendous amount of time we had both been spending emailing each other from work, and I bought his explanation. I was sure my boss would be happy if my productivity increased, so I shrugged it off and didn't think about it much more.

The next Saturday, I nervously began preparing for dinner. I planned something nice, but it needed to be something that could not burn. I chose minestrone soup and salad. I also stocked up on plenty of beer in case either one of us needed a little extra liquid courage. I was very nervous about cooking for him again and had a few beers to loosen up while I chopped things for the salad and waited for him to come over. The beer calmed my nerves.

I was floored when Michael arrived and he was wearing a pair of old gym shorts and his Denver Broncos football jersey. I, on the other hand, had put the effort into dressing up and wore a skirt and blouse.

His first comment when he came through the door was, "Sorry, babe. I guess I came a little under-dressed. I thought we were just having a quiet night at home, but you do look beautiful."

I responded to him with a deep kiss and said with a wink, "Maybe it won't be too long before neither one of us will be wearing clothes."

I was hell-bent on trying to keep the mood light and put him at ease. But even as I aimed at lightheartedness, something inside me sensed that his laugh was a little forced. I felt a twinge of something off-balance between us, but I chose to ignore my instincts.

He came in the house and headed straight to the couch and sat down, obviously assuming I was going to bring him a beer. He was already getting pretty comfortable being in my house, and his relaxation put me at ease. When I brought in the beer, I sat down on the couch, leaned in for a kiss, and handed him his drink. My intuition still told me something was off, but his kisses were warm and inviting, and I decided to ignore my unease yet again.

We sat on the couch and talked casually for about twenty minutes, waiting for the minestrone to warm up, and sharing stories about our daily events. I loved sitting on my couch with Michael's arms around me. No matter what, he always made me feel safe and secure when we were cuddling.

Michael was a great storyteller. He loved to make me laugh and to impress me with his prestige at work.

As soon as the timer went off, I went to the kitchen and served dinner. Teasingly, I bragged about how proud I was of myself for not burning the soup. We both laughed as we got our plates together and went into the other room to sit down for dinner. It was nice to have a man around who was willing to do simple things like grab the salad dressing out of the refrigerator and put it on the table. I was comfortable having Michael help me around the house.

During dinner, everything seemed normal. It reminded me of the fantasies I had of us where this type of "normal" activity occurred every day. We hadn't been seeing each other for very long, and yet I had already begun to build the dream of living the rest of my life with this man.

After dinner, he helped me clear the dishes, and I packed the leftovers to send home with him. I'd completely forgotten he'd said he wanted to talk. Unconsciously, I hoped that whatever upset him had already blown over. No such luck.

Once we settled back down on the couch, he looked at me with big, sad brown eyes, and I could tell whatever troubled him was bothering him deeply.

The next words out of his mouth were, "You deserve someone better than me."

I felt shocked, and I'm sure I looked at him like he was crazy. I could not begin to fathom what he meant. As far as my feelings went, I was sitting there with the perfect man. How could he possibly think I wanted someone better? I started to speak up when he asked me to let him finish before I spoke again.

He went on. "I'm sorry, Sue, but no matter what happens between us, I will never be able to openly acknowledge you to my Native American family and friends. The Indian world can never know about us."

He said he'd been thinking all week about how he was going to tell me how he truly felt. He explained when he first met me he was looking for someone with whom to have a little fun. He was totally caught off guard by how deeply we connected and how quickly it had happened, but he could not allow himself to get any more deeply involved with me.

He said he'd known that he had to make me understand his feelings when I had told him the week before that I wanted to go watch him emcee a powwow. He did his best to explain to me that could never happen. He told me he would never be ready to introduce me to any of his friends or his family, and he knew that it was not fair to me.

He went on to clarify just how angry and judgmental Native Americans were towards white people. He elaborated that Native American women, in particular, hated it when white women dated their Native American men, and their disdain became heightened when the man was a successful Native American like him. He rationalized that, because of his elder status, his relationship and loyalty to the Native American community was now one of his greatest responsibilities. He said he doubted that I could understand, but he had just turned fifty years old, and now he was considered an elder in the community. It was incumbent on him to protect his role and responsibilities. He had tears in his eyes when he looked at me and said, "I will completely understand if you never want to see me again; but after tonight, I won't discuss this topic ever again."

I was glued to my couch, immobilized and stunned. One voice in my head wanted to scream, "Get the hell out of my house and out of my life!"

But another overwhelming part of my brain could not—and would not—accept what he was telling me. I silently vacillated between, "I can change his mind," and, "I am willing to live with whatever rules he creates." Of course, deep down I had a belief that I was unworthy of love and true happiness, but at the time I was not consciously aware of this old, old belief. Some subconscious part of me was willing to accept that no matter what restrictions the relationship held, he was the best man who would ever come my way. I also believed, deeply in my subconscious, I could change his mind.

For a few minutes, I just sat and stared at him. I wasn't exactly sure what to say or what to do, but it didn't take me long to make a decision that would affect the next several years of my life. I leaned over to him and kissed him passionately. I was not consciously aware that I had just settled for much less than I deserved. I said, "I will take you in whatever ways I can have you, for as long as I can have you."

He looked at me and said, "Good answer," and sighed like it was a huge relief. The next thing I knew, I was following him into my bedroom to begin my first unconscious attempt to change his mind.

After we'd made love and I was lying in his arms, attempting to process what had just happened, I decided to broach the powwow subject again. Thinking about our last conversation, I told him I wanted to see him emcee the powwow in the town of Golden in a few weeks. I tried to explain to him that no matter what, I still wanted to experience a powwow. This one would be outside in a public place, and it seemed like the perfect opportunity for me to discreetly observe the event.

He said, "I can't stop you from going, but now you know the rules: I will not talk to you or acknowledge that I know you, if you show up."

I laid there in his arms trying to digest whether or not he was serious. I knew he wasn't joking, but I just couldn't imagine that he wouldn't at least say, "Hi." I didn't expect him to walk up and throw his arms around me, but surely he would at least talk to me?

I pondered our entire conversation over the next few

days and thought specifically about what not ever being publically acknowledged by him would mean for our future. I kept debating with myself about whether or not it would be good for me to go to the powwow.

Finally, I came to the conclusion that I wanted to go to the damn powwow, but I didn't want to go by myself. I decided to ask a friend to go with me.

Part of me was aware, in that moment, that I wasn't telling myself the full truth. Once again I was putting someone else's wishes, wants, and desires above my own.

CHAPTER 8

— ♪ —

I drove to Wanda's house to pick her up on the day of the powwow, as my internal debate persisted about whether or not to go. I wondered whether taking her was in my best interest. I desperately wanted to go, and to have a friend with me felt like a great idea. She seemed like a good choice to me because she was already deeply involved and living with a Native American man. I assumed she'd already traversed this road, and she seemed happy, so I thought she would be a good ally to have.

The downside in going anywhere with my friend Wanda was how self-conscious and intimidated I felt around her because of her beauty. She is the kind of woman who walks into a room, and every head turns to admire her. She's tall, with a body-builder figure. She has long, flowing brown hair and has the perfect mixture of Eurasian features. If she weren't such a good friend, I could easily have been resentful of her, based purely on her external looks. The upside of her going, though, was that if I were to be with someone who got all of the attention, my short, fat, dumpy body could remain invisible. I didn't want to risk standing out in the crowd.

It felt safe to me to have someone else absorb all of the attention while I invisibly observed and figured out exactly what the Native American community was like. I wasn't worried about her being in competition with me for Michael's attention. After all, she was already involved, and I was pretty sure Michael would not be anyone she found interesting in a romantic way.

As we were getting ready to leave for the powwow, Wanda, her boyfriend Gene, and I stood out in their driveway chatting. I wanted to engage Gene into a conversation. I was dying to know what he thought about everything Michael had said to me about the Native community not being open to white women dating Indian men. I needed to figure out a way to ask my questions without making either of them uncomfortable.

Gene had grown up around an Indian Reservation, and although he was not active in the Denver Indian community, I thought maybe he could give me some insight into Michael's decision.

I stood there and fidgeted and finally decided to just ask him if it was ever an issue for him to date a white woman. Wanda looked at me rather strangely, and I thought, "Oh my God. I've just crossed into some forbidden territory."

He said, "What are you talking about?"

I kind of stammered my way through explaining to him what Michael had told me. I had a hard time repeating the words Michael had used because the issue was so close to me and talking about it already made my heart hurt. I hoped Wanda had already shared my situation with him because I had told her about Michael's decision, and she had said she was going to talk to him about it. Apparently, that had not happened.

I tried to keep it as simple as possible and just explained what Michael told me about Native Americans beings so prejudiced against white people. I tried to explain that Michael was afraid the Denver Native American community would disown him if he openly dated me.

The more I tried to explain what Michael said, the more Gene told me he just didn't get Michael's reasoning. To him, it sounded like old, outdated thinking. He went on to elaborate that he understood where the prejudice came from, but was surprised to hear it in Denver. He said many older Indians are still very angry about what happened to their ancestors but most younger people had moved on.

Gene wondered aloud if Michael was testing me to make sure I wasn't just another white person trying to come in and usurp the Native American traditions. He knew it made a lot of Native American elders angry when white people tried to get information from their secret societies.

I told him about a conversation that Michael and I had the previous week when Michael asked me if I could explain to him why white people were so enthralled with Native American culture. Michael's question had caught me off guard because, although I had been a spiritual seeker for many years, I hadn't been drawn specifically to Native American spirituality. Up until meeting Michael, I was probably much more interested in different forms of "Magick" and had a small amount of knowledge about

Wicca and white witchcraft. I had adopted the philosophy of "do no harm" and believed firmly that every action (whether your intention was good or bad) would come back to you three-fold.

When Michael and I talked about spirituality, it had not occurred to me he thought I might be looking for insight into his Native traditions. Native American spirituality was the furthest thing from my mind then. I understood it was part of who he was, and would obviously come with the whole package, but it was my physical attraction to him and how he made me feel that kept me interested in Michael.

As we stood there, Wanda told me she was surprised I wasn't bothered by not being able to approach Michael at the powwow that afternoon. She thought it was one of the craziest things she'd ever heard, but she knew it was important to me so she would play along.

I asked Gene if his culture was ever an issue for them, and he told me it had never crossed his mind. But he also reminded me that he didn't interact a lot with Native Americans since he had moved to Denver. The three of us decided it might have been different because of Michael's position as a leader in the community and his new status as an elder. He wished me luck and told us to have fun. I asked him if he wanted to come with us, and he laughed and just said, "No, thanks." I felt encouraged by his words as we headed off on our adventure.

I've always been an organized planner, so I'd already looked up the address for the park where the powwow was being held. It would have been hard to miss with all the cars. It was a nice cool afternoon, and although the sun was shining, the part of the park that was holding the powwow was shaded.

We arrived about twenty minutes before it was supposed to start, but Michael had already explained the concept of "Indian time" to me. He said, "At the beginning of time, whenever that was, Indians didn't wear a watch." Time didn't have the same meaning to them, and they rarely start any event on time.

I asked him how that concept of time worked for him when he worked in a regular job. He explained he had learned to be punctual in the military, but most of his Indian friends and family don't believe in linear time. They prefer to allow things just to unfold more naturally. That being said, I was not at all surprised when the start time came and went, and we were still standing there waiting.

As they got ready to begin, I could hear Michael's voice over the loudspeaker across the park. As the emcee, he was front and center. Frankly, it would've been tough to miss a 6'4" 375-pound man, whether his voice boomed over the microphone in his hand or not. He had told me it was his job as emcee to explain to both the crowd and the Indians what was happening and to keep the event going. I knew being the emcee was something very important to him because it kept him connected to his community, and it was an additional small source of income.

As we walked around the park, I noticed quite a few other white people were also there watching, so I didn't feel quite so conspicuous. I had given Michael my word that I would not walk up to him or approach him in any way, so instead I found a perfect place to stand and watch his every move without being terribly obvious.

I found the bright colors of all of the different outfits interesting and was a little surprised that Michael wore a maroon-colored dress shirt with a bolo tie and a black sports jacket. I knew he owned an Indian outfit because he wore it in the very first picture he sent me. I guess I just assumed he would wear that to every powwow.

Watching him from a distance had its advantages. I noticed he kept looking around, and that he was trying to be subtle about it. He had no idea we were already there, but I think he sensed he was being watched. We were playing a game, and oddly, although it was his game and his rules, part of me still wanted to beat him at it.

I was content just watching him. It felt a little like observing and tracking an animal in its natural habitat before placing the snare. I wasn't trying to get his attention, but it did not take long for him to scan the crowd and find where we were standing. When our eyes met, he gave me a very subtle nod and turned around to talk to someone else. Although we had made our agreement, I was still a little disappointed he hadn't made more eye contact. At least he was aware I had arrived.

The sights and sounds enthralled me. The Indians—tall, short, fat, thin, young, and old—were clothed in breathtaking buckskin dresses and colorful shawls. Both men and women wore elaborate beading, many of them in outfits of pieces of silky material in vibrant red, deep pink, sparkling green, effervescent yellow, and bright orange.

Many men had large bells around their ankles that rang as they walked. One of the most striking sights was a woman the same size as me, in a beautiful pale blue outfit, with a matching shawl decorated with exquisite beading and embroidery. Seeing another plus size woman who was obviously accepted and honored despite her size comforted me. Maybe he wasn't lying when he said my size wasn't an issue. The issue that remained was the color of my skin, and ironically it was something I could not change. I didn't know whether to be thrilled because I didn't have to strive to lose weight to please him or be pissed because my skin tone was not anything I had control over.

I knew most of Michael's friends and family were going to be there that day, and I was curious to see how each of them dressed and how they looked. I especially wanted to see Michael's brother, Lance. Michael had made it very clear in the first few weeks we'd known each other that Lance was somebody very important in his life. I could hardly wait to see him, even if it was going to be from a distance. The challenge was trying to figure out which one was Lance.

CHAPTER 9

— ♪ —

When it was time for the actual ceremony to start, Michael asked all the participants to get into line for Grand Entry, and asked the audience to stand. Next, he invited the host drum to play an "honor song," and they responded with a beautiful drumbeat. Although they were singing, it sounded more like guttural chanting. I had no idea what the words meant, but it touched my heart. I was mesmerized and spent the next several minutes watching Indians move to the beat of the drum as they entered the arena.

The first people to enter the circle were a group of uniformed men who stood proud as if they were marching in somewhat of a military formation. These men carried an Eagle Staff, an American Flag, and a MIA POW flag into the center of the arena. Several dozen elderly people followed the uniformed men. Some of these men wore baseball caps with veteran insignia. The women of the group were either dressed in traditional outfits or wore beautiful shawls over their everyday clothes.

Behind the elders was a group of beautiful young women wearing what looked like beauty-pageant sashes that read "Princess," each one representing a specific tribe. Behind the royalty were men in colorful traditional attire, most of them wearing feathers or headbands, followed by women in beautiful buckskin dresses with fancy shawls. Some women were wearing dresses decorated with dozens of hand-sewn ornaments that jingled as they moved. The young, male teen dancers, followed by the young female dancers, followed the older women next in the procession. Finally, at the very end, was a group of adorable young children—both boys and girls—in miniature versions of the adult outfits. Some of them were too small to walk and were being carried by their parents. It was surprising to me that even the little two-year-olds called "Tiny Tots" already had a sense of rhythm. As they came into the arena, they were being taught the traditions of entering the sacred powwow circle.

Dancers of all ages filled the arena, and the majority of them wore breathtaking Native outfits in hues of many bright colors. The spectacular sight was both exciting and beautiful. The majesty truly moved my heart. At that moment, I began to see why being an active part of the powwow circuit was vitally important to Michael.

Once the last Grand Entry song played, the flags were posted by the announcer stand, and everyone cleared the arena. Michael declared the next dance would be an intertribal dance where all of the participants were invited into the main circle to dance. It was fascinating to see all of the different costumes and watch the grace of their movements as each person danced to the rhythm of the drum. My friend and I agreed their dancing was impressive.

The only thing that kept it from being a perfect experience was my being kept from approaching or talking to Michael. It was challenging to stand thirty feet away and not be able to at least say, "Hello." I had given him my word that I would not approach. As a way to appease myself, I justified in my mind that he was working—that he was an on-stage performer—and I couldn't bother him at work. The justification made sense to me and was enough to keep me from walking up and throwing my arms around his neck and kissing him.

We watched several more dances. Most of the time, both Wanda and I were enthralled with the way the Indians performed. It didn't take long before we realized they had arranged the dancers by type of dance and were having contests to see who the best dancer was. Each type of dance had a different feel and a different type of costume. I particularly loved the traditional male dancers and the jingle-dress women dancers. It was fascinating to watch them twirl around to the rhythm of the music.

A little while later, Michael announced his brother Lance would be leading a men's traditional dance. I had been dying to figure out who Lance was. I had it narrowed down to about five guys when Michael finally said something to him over the loud speaker. Lance appeared in full traditional regalia, and I quickly realized that not only was Lance extremely physically attractive, but his inner spirit showed in the grace of his movement. Watching him dance affected something deep inside of me. His spiritual presence exuded from every pore of his body as he danced around the arena.

As soon as that dance was over, Michael jokingly announced, "You'd better watch out brother; there's people from the Arapahoe County Sheriff's Office here looking to arrest you." As he made this announcement, Michael laughed and laughed. Everyone in the crowd thought it was a big joke, but he looked at me grinning and winked. It was the first of many times that Michael said things over the PA system I knew were directed specifically to me. It made my skin tingle to know he had sort of gone against his own rules and acknowledged my presence. Wanda looked at me with a confused expression and asked what that was about, and I just shrugged and smiled. I later realized it was the best he could do to acknowledge me without acknowledging me. At that moment, it was enough.

After we had watched several more dances, we walked around and looked at the dozen or so vendor booths. I hadn't expected there to be items for sale, so I hadn't brought a lot of cash with me. Most of the booths were selling beautiful pieces of jewelry obviously handmade by the people selling them, but oddly, none of them had price tags. I was curious as to whether or not they would barter. In the end, when I found a pair of sterling silver buffalo earrings, I wanted them so badly I just paid her what she asked for them. My friend wondered if I could have talked the woman down in price, but I was afraid if I tried to barter I wouldn't get the ones I wanted.

Wanda asked me why that particular pair of earrings was important to me and I explained to her Michael's Indian name was Tatanka Wiscobe, which meant "buffalo man" to his Otoe-Missouria tribe, and he considered buffaloes his true brothers and sisters. I'm not sure if she understood what I was explaining, but she nodded her head in agreement, and we moved on to see what else was available.

We were moving through the crowd, and I looked up and saw Lance walking toward us. As he approached, his eyes were locked on me as though my beautiful friend were invisible. He looked directly at me and only said, "Hello," but in a way that I felt as if he was glad to see me. Although he'd just kept walking, his simple word cemented himself permanently in my heart. He would never know how his acknowledgment of me in that moment affected me.

I'd spent the last fifteen years watching men fall all over themselves to get my beautiful friend Wanda's attention, because she is a stunning woman. I just assumed Lance would notice her long before he noticed me, but instead he completely ignored her. It felt like Lance saw through the barriers I had put up to the world with my physical body and could truly see the beauty of my soul. Michael was still the brother I wanted to be with, but I sensed that Lance was someone truly remarkable, and even though he merely walked past us, he had made a huge first impression.

As the day went on, I became more adept at putting faces to the names of the people Michael had talked about the last few weeks. After learning who his brother was, it was easier to identify the other members of his drumming group and his close friends. Although Michael was emcee, he told me he was also a member of the Colorado Intertribal Drum Group. He explained Colorado Intertribal is a

"Southern" drum, which meant they play during dances more specific to the Southern region Indians. He'd told me there would be times he would sit down at the drum with his group and sing, and I looked forward to hearing them.

Michael told me both before the powwow, and then announced over the PA system, that Tracy Martinez makes the best Indian Fry Bread known to mankind. After we had been there a while, I was still trying to figure out who Tracy Martinez was because somehow I felt threatened by Tracy's cooking abilities. But I couldn't figure it out, and I hate to admit it, but my jealousy quotient ran pretty damn high. I'd never eaten Indian Fry Bread, and I wanted to try what Michael had been raving about, specifically that which was made by Tracy. There was only one food vendor, but there were several people behind the counter putting together mounds of dough and deep frying them, while others turned them into Indian Tacos made with the infamous Indian fry bread, a delicious combination of fried dough, beans, lettuce and cheese.

My brain spent almost an hour trying to figure out how in the hell I was going to be able to determine which person in that booth was Tracy. By some telepathy or just a pure coincidence, Michael called Tracy Martinez to the speaker stand. Much to my absolute amazement—Tracy Martinez was a MAN.

I laughed out loud to the point that a few people around me kind of looked at me sideways. I had inadvertently let out a little "whoop" when I realized my self-invented competition was with a 45-year-old married man, not a beautiful Indian princess. I had even conjured up a story in my head that Tracy's cooking meant she would steal Michael's heart. My insecurities ran so deep they'd almost gotten the better of me! I was grateful I hadn't done anything to let Michael know how jealous I was before I figured it all out.

Watching the powwow was a lot of fun, yet when it was over I was still very disappointed Michael never approached us. The most startling contact I had with him was when he mentioned my agency over the loud speaker. I had more contact with his brother Lance, in passing, than I had with Michael.

Still, I was happy because I felt like I finally understood more of what Michael told me about his heritage and why the powwow circuit was very important to him.

CHAPTER 10

— ♪ —

Because of our schedules, it was two weeks after the powwow in Golden before Michael and I could see each other again. From March to October, almost every weekend he was committed to participate in different powwows around the region. Most of the time he was the emcee, sometimes he danced, the rest of the time he went to sing and hang out with his drum group.

I would often go and observe the powwows around Denver, which somehow made it easier to go longer periods without seeing him one-on-one. Michael usually spoke to me in "code" over the loud speaker to let me know he knew I was there. We had gotten back to emailing a lot during the day and sending instant messages at night. Once I accepted the conditions of our relationship, the lines of communication were completely re-opened, and I pretended I felt satisfied.

I even began to imagine I was slowly being introduced to and allowed deeper into his inner world, even though we didn't see each other as frequently, and his friends and family still didn't know anything about me. At least I was getting to know more about him and his beliefs.

More importantly, I got more comfortable with the idea of allowing him to love me. I knew the situation wasn't ideal, but that was counter-balanced from my joy over the attentiveness he lavished on me when we were together. It was the greatest tenderness I had ever received from a man.

Most of our communication was still in written form. We only talked on the phone every few days. When we did talk, we usually spent a couple of hours discussing a wide variety of topics that allowed each of us to see more intimately into the other. Conversation came easily to both of us. Michael told me stories about his childhood, about his friends and family, and kept me informed on what was happening at his job. Most of his stories made me laugh. I loved his cynical and sarcastic sense of humor because it mirrored mine. We would swap stories about the people we worked with, and we'd laugh about how incompetent some of our bosses and co-workers seemed to be.

Michael loved his job. Their organization provided contracted security for numerous companies and Michael was often responsible for more than one building site. He'd tell me stories about the people he watched on security cameras doing inappropriate things with no idea they were being watched.

One of my favorite stories was about a woman who kept sneaking over to a co-worker's desk and eating his candy, then she would sit in meetings and talk about how disgusting she thought candy was and how well her latest diet worked. This sneaking, eating, and downplaying went on for a couple of weeks because it wasn't a security issue. It just annoyed Michael.

One day he asked her to stop by his desk on her way out of the office and showed her the camera footage from that day. It was no secret the cameras were in place, but she was mortified at being caught. He laughed for six months about the expression on her face and how she would no longer look at him when she came in the building. He would call her Miss Twix to me. I never did know her real name, but when he left that particular building site, she still worked there, and neither one of us were surprised she'd never warmed back up to him.

Occasionally I would take lunch to him at work. It was ironic that I could visit him at work as much as I wanted because he didn't care if the white people he worked with knew he was dating me.

Frequently, his stories were more about his friends and families than himself. I loved hearing about his brother Lance, because he made such an impression on me the first time I saw him. He was my favorite member of Michael's family, which sounds strange because I knew Lance had no idea who I was, but I held hope someday that could change.

Michael helped me understand how Native American lineage works by explaining Lance was part Cheyenne, part Comanche, and part Kiowa. Lance had a strong lineage as a descendant of two chiefs, Chief Wildhorse and Chief Jacob Allrunner. Lance's Indian name was Nakose, meaning Little Bear, although most of the time his family referred to him as "Bubba."

Lance was a member of both the Cheyenne Dog Soldier Society and the Bald Eagle Society. He also was a Sun Dancer and participated in a lot of Native American ceremonies across the region. At the time, he worked as a family caseworker at the Denver Indian Family Resource Center and always involved himself with things that helped the Indian youth of the community.

It didn't take long for me to realize Lance was a prominent member of the Native American world and a very spiritual man. After I had heard numerous stories about him, it became obvious that Lance was much more comfortable in the Native American world than he was in the "white man's world." Michael on the other hand had become very adept and comfortable in both worlds.

Lance also had a deep, authentic, heart-felt need to help others. There were times I wished Lance and I could become good friends because of our similar views on helping the oppressed. For many reasons, I held out hope that Lance and I would have a chance to get acquainted with one another.

One night, Michael was upset because he heard a couple of the younger guys at a powwow call him an "apple" behind his back. I thought he was mad because they thought he was fat. As it turns out, "apple" is a derogative term for a Native American who looks "red" (Native) on the outside and "white" on the inside. He told me it confirmed his beliefs about why he would never take a white woman to an Indian event. They already thought he had turned "too white," and openly dating me would just exacerbate their judgment of him. Although his feelings hurt my heart, I was used to compartmentalizing my needs and beliefs and just chose to go along for the sake of getting along and not losing him.

I knew Michael needed to feel completely accepted in the Indian community. I was frustrated because it seemed like for every two steps forward I made in convincing him it would be okay to introduce me into his world, he took three steps backward. But instead of voicing my frustration, I stuffed my feelings and reassured him that I was fine going to the Indian events and just observing. My self-esteem was so low I pretended it was acceptable for me to live by his rules. I was afraid that after the comment about "Apple," he would no longer want me to attend other powwows.

As it turned out, because I told him I understood, he shared with me about an event where he was announcing a Gourd Dance. The Gourd Dance would be held before the actual start of a powwow and was considered a separate activity. The Gourd Dance is a celebration dance just for men. Women are allowed to participate only by dancing in place behind their men outside of the perimeter. Michael explained the Kiowas started the Gourd Dance, and because his best friend was a Kiowa Indian, Michael was invited to join the Kiowa Gourd Dance Society.

The Society was formed based on an old tale. The Kiowa believe a young man became separated from his tribe, and one day when he was hungry and dehydrated after many days of trying to find his way back, he heard an unusual kind of singing. When he sought out who was singing, he found a big red wolf singing and dancing on its hind legs. The man watched and listened to the songs all night. In the morning, the wolf spoke to him and told him to take the songs back to the Kiowa people, and then the wolf showed him which direction to travel.

The best way to identify a Gourd Dance song is by the howl at the end of the song that is a tribute to the red wolf that saved the man.

I found the Gourd Dance fascinating to watch. Similar to a powwow, the men danced in a circle. Each woman was only allowed to stand behind her man and sway to the music. During the majority of the dance, the men simply stood in place and lifted their feet in time to the drumbeat. Each dancer carried a rattle, and occasionally one of the men would wander a few feet into the circle and turn around and go back to where he had been standing.

The costumes were different, too. Everyone appeared dressed in a similar way. The majority of the people in attendance wore regular street clothes, but there was a dark colored sash tied at their waist, and then a blanket-like shawl was placed over their shoulders. The shawl was red on one end and blue on the other, and all of the dancers wore the red on the same side. Most of the guys had on either cowboy hats or baseball caps. There weren't any Native American headdresses worn.

I was fascinated to see a group of men stand in a circle and simply step to a beat without moving while they softly shook their rattles. The gourd dance was about ninety minutes and as soon as it was over, they started the powwow. As I sat and watched Michael and Lance and their friends, I couldn't help wonder if there would ever be a time I would be allowed to stand behind Michael while he danced.

CHAPTER 11

— ❧ —

Every few weeks, I'd let Michael know I wouldn't be available to email him much during the day. I had work to complete away from my office. I was responsible for maintaining my own agency's policies and procedures, and doing internal accreditation compliance Staff Inspections.

A big part of my job was also making sure our agency policy manual stayed up to date with the revisions the CALEA standards. When a new standard arrived, it was up to me to draft the policy to meet the standard in a way the members of the agency could tolerate. I labored hours over each and every policy written. Typically I created a draft policy and presented the draft to the people responsible for the function involved before presenting to command staff for final approval.

Command staff meetings occurred once a week. It was typically a three-hour meeting with the top management of the agency. The sheriff, undersheriff, two bureau chiefs, four captains, and the Budget Manager would meet to discuss what was happening in the agency.

Under the previous sheriff, I had been considered an actual member of command staff. In time, the new sheriff changed the command structure and excluded me. Suddenly, I was only allowed to go in and present the drafted policy at the beginnings of the meeting and was asked to leave before a discussion about any sensitive information could begin. It was a pretty big ego hit when I was only allowed to attend the part of the meetings that discussed policy. The other topics of the meeting were suddenly considered too sensitive for me. The new administration was very different from the previous one, and it took a while for me to understand and accept my new, lesser role in the process.

Once the policies were approved and distributed, I used a Staff Inspection process to verify that the policies were being followed. The intent was to make sure all personnel were following agency policies and procedures. The Staff Inspection position was initially created to be filled by a sworn deputy inspector. It was needed to meet an accreditation requirement, but because of budget cuts it was eventually added to my responsibilities as Accreditation Manager. I accepted the additional responsibility because it wouldn't be acceptable for me to be out inspecting other agencies' compliance with National Standards and have it come to light that my own agency wasn't following its policies. At that time, I still took my job very seriously.

The Staff Inspection process was laborious. The process started with a review of the applicable national standards and our agency policy, and ended with observing and interviewing employees.

The people I interacted with were normally very friendly to my face, but for years I had heard the things they said behind my back. Once again, ignoring these rumors was a defense mechanism. It was impossible to be a complete people-pleaser when I was getting someone in trouble for not doing his or her job correctly, yet I always strove to make other people happy.

At the time I had no idea what the stress of the job did to my inner world. I just built up the armor of my body and created an internal prison to hide my true feelings.

Ironically, I didn't actually have the authority to enforce the policy. I could only identify the areas where the policy was being ignored and pass that information up the chain-of-command, or occasionally directly to the sheriff. Unfortunately, having direct access to the sheriff never helped me make friends at work. Because everyone knew I had the authority to "rat them out," I was perceived as someone "running to the boss" with every little discrepancy.

Even with the changes in administration in 2002, my peers still saw me as a member of command staff with a direct line to the sheriff. This misinformed belief still affected the way people interacted with me. When I look back at my career, I see where I had subconsciously chosen to stay in a profession in which being invisible and emotionally shutdown was an acceptable defense mechanism. This was just one more example of the many times in my life when I felt like the little girl standing outside the window, looking in at the big boys having fun. It was similar to the feelings I had when I attended powwows—over the years I'd just become used to being the observer and not being allowed to participate.

Going out and inspecting how well other people performed their jobs endeared me to neither staff or management. Many perceived me to be motivated to catch them doing things wrong, but really, all I wanted to do was document that they were following policy. I truly hated conflict, and wondered how in the hell I'd ever gotten into the position of inspecting other people. My aversion to conflict compounded the irony of being in a position where my level of influence was perceived to be elevated. In reality, I didn't have the authority to change what others were doing. No one in the new administration wanted me to find any actual violations. They seemed to prefer for me to say everything was okay, so they could continue to maintain the status quo.

Even more challenging for me was that I no longer felt part of either the command staff or the other personnel. It was a lonely existence because I felt excluded from both. I was good at masking my feelings, so I don't think anyone ever noticed how miserable I'd become.

In reality, if I'd had more self-confidence and the backing of the new administration when conducting the inspections, all types of issues might have been revealed long before they were eventually brought to light.

I often sat in front my computer, so I could easily stay in touch with Michael. Most of the time, I split screens and answered his emails while I prepared for and documented the inspections. My time away from my computer actually conducting an inspection was the only time when my relationship with Michael was interrupted.

My position at this point reported directly to the captain

in charge of Internal Affairs. Sadly, most of the agency just assumed I was a spy for both Internal Affairs and the sheriff. Over the years, I got used to people shutting up when I walked into a room. I tried to convince them how mistaken they were, but it didn't help. Whenever I found a significant policy violation, I had to report it.

I vacillated between feeling torn from wanting my co-workers to like me and maintaining my professional reputation. Most of the time, worry over my reputation won the battle. There were people who liked me, and most understood I was just doing my job.

For years, I'd focused all of my time and energy toward my career. I look back now and see I had become a workaholic, and, as a result, I no longer had a social life. My dad had modeled this work ethic while I was growing up. His job always came first. Subconsciously, not only had I entered into law enforcement and taken on a life of trying to please him, I adopted his strong work ethic, which actually translated to workaholism for each of us.

Before I met Michael, I worked nine to eleven hour days, often six days a week. Forgetting my dad's deathbed advice about the new sheriff, I still had visions of being re-accepted as a member of command staff. I believed I just needed to strive a little harder; therefore my work would get the sheriff and our agency positive attention.

I felt conflicted professionally. I was being removed from a position of influence by the current administration. During that same time, however, I continued to stay involved in special interest groups attached to the CALEA Commission where I still enjoyed great respect.

I continued to be appointed to subcommittees responsible for creating national standards. When I was away from my agency, I had a seat at the table and a strong voice among law-enforcement executives from around North America. Ironically, in my own agency, I was being quietly dismissed from any powerful conversations.

The new sheriff had also been an assessor for CALEA before his election, and, initially, I thought it would be a great benefit to me. Just as I had, he had traveled the country inspecting other agencies. I wasn't surprised when, within a year of being elected sheriff, he started working towards an appointed position on the Commission itself, and, sure enough, he was chosen to sit on the Commission.

Much to my surprise, once he joined the Commission, I felt more and more obsolete within my agency. My travel budget to Commission conferences was reduced, and other members of command staff became certified as assessors. At first, I was excited to have others joining me while inspecting agencies. It didn't take long before I was being bypassed in the selection process for the guys who carried a badge and gun and held the title of Captain.

To make my life even more interesting, the guys at the top no longer needed me to interpret standards, yet my co-workers were still threatened by my presence. It was nice to have Michael in my life to understand and support me emotionally, because I could tell him about a lot of the dirty politics I was seeing around me.

Although he still kept our relationship a secret from the Indian community, he frequently sat and listened to me for hours and gave me advice on how to handle agency politics. He would say, "Mark my words, everything that man does will come back to bite him in the ass someday."

Part of me hoped he was right. Mostly, I believed that my life was stuck right where it was.

CHAPTER 12

— ✺ —

Michael and I fell into a consistent pattern. We emailed each other first thing in the morning, but not quite as regularly throughout the day. We still spent a lot of time on AOL Instant Messenger at night. We typically had dinner together once a week, alternating between a restaurant and my house. Of course the restaurants we went to were only places where he knew none of his Indian friends would go to. It had begun to feel like our normal routine, and I didn't question our arrangement as much. I pretended it was enough for me to just have a man who loved me, someone who made love to me unlike anyone I had ever experienced, and kept me stimulated intellectually by sharing all of his spiritual beliefs.

He also gave me beautiful gifts. I'll always cherish both the Pendleton blanket he gave me for my birthday right after we met and the purple star quilt he had made for me a couple of years later.

As much as I secretly continued to want Michael to stand up and acknowledge me in the Native community, I had become somewhat content with the way our lives blended.

It became easier for me to watch him interacting with his friends and family at powwows and other Native gatherings. Sometimes I took a friend with me, but most of the time I just went by myself. It was easier to move around the event that way, and I could leave if I became too uncomfortable.

Sometimes it felt strange because, while we were together, I began to feel like I knew the people I saw on a fairly regular basis. I would sit at their events knowing so much about them, but restricted by Michael from interacting with them. I heard many stories about Lance and many other members of Michael's community. None of them had a clue who I was. I could have walked up to them and not only known their names, but also where they worked, their children's names, and other tidbits of information about their lives.

Michael repeatedly told me about the latest Denver Indian Center gossip, and he enjoyed sharing the gossip he heard around the older Native women. He cackled when he described how they interrelated with one another. I felt like part of the community, but oddly, they didn't know it.

Part of me continued to believe it was only a matter of time before Michael would change his mind, stand up, and introduce me. I daydreamed that his friends and family would be impressed with how quickly I learned about them and remembered their names, and that somehow, someway, that would make them like me.

Some of my favorite conversations with Michael were about Native American traditions, especially around Lance's spiritual rituals. Although Michael was spiritual and followed many Native American traditions, Lance's beliefs were much deeper and more impactful. Those conversations gave me a false belief that he was trying to prepare me for involvement in his culture. I was enthralled by his stories and usually imagined what it would be like to feel included in some of the ceremonies he described. All these dreams occurred in my mind alone, because I didn't dare give them a voice to Michael.

I also wondered what Lance would think if he knew about everything Michael shared with me. Michael once said he would just deny ever having told me anything, and I believed him, but it didn't stop my fantasy-world thinking. At that point, the likelihood of my ever having a conversation with Lance was so unlikely it felt like a non-issue.

One of my favorite topics of conversation was around Michael's belief in "little spirit people." He wouldn't talk about this often, but over time he convinced me there are actually "little spirit people" around all the time. At first I thought he was teasing me. We would be sitting on the couch talking, and he would point to something in the corner and say, "Did you see that one?"

After a while, especially when I was home alone in a quiet house, I would notice little tiny movements. Sometimes they appeared as specks of light, but it was usually just something moving very quickly. I don't know how many times I thought I had mice running in my house before I finally started to believe in his "little spirit people" theory.

Michael also believed in shape-shifting, but I wondered

whether or not it was real. He explained he was out camping in the woods and saw people shift into animals, birds, and insects. The story he told me happened when he was a little boy, and his grandfather had taken him to an encampment of some sort. He wasn't supposed to get up and go outside during the night. Once though, when he had to pee, he snuck out to the wooded area and saw a young man change into a four-legged animal. He said that he didn't believe his own eyes, and he ran back to his blankets and crawled back under as fast he possibly could. The next morning, he asked his grandfather about it and before he could finish his sentence, his grandfather looked at him and harshly said, "Never speak of that to me again."

I felt honored when Michael trusted me enough to tell me those stories, but part of me wondered if it was something he made up. I think he believed the stories he told me. I have not seen it myself, but I do believe anything is possible. Just because I have not seen it, does not mean it can't happen.

When we weren't talking about spirituality, we talked about politics. He was an active member of the American Indian Movement (AIM) and voiced very strong feelings about what the American government had done for hundreds of years to Native Americans. There were times when I cringed as he recounted the things that happened to him over the years. I was most shocked at the story of him being spat on at work.

With Michael being such a big man, I could hardly believe someone actually had the courage to spit in his eye and call him a "savage." What made it worse was that it had happened when he worked as a security guard at a hospital in the eighties, and the other man involved was a fellow employee. Someone saw it and reported it, yet nothing was ever done. He chalked it up to just one of many instances of prejudice he frequently had to face based on his ancestry.

I had not been directly affected by prejudice in my life prior to meeting Michael. He opened my eyes to how a person could be judged just by the color of his or her skin and his or her ancestry. At the time Michael was telling me these stories, ironically enough, he believed his peers would discriminate against me based solely on my heritage. I found it ironic that it was my skin color that kept him from openly dating me in his community.

No matter what he said, I continued to dream that eventually he would change his mind and recognize that I could fit into his world as well as he had learned to fit into the white man's world.

CHAPTER 13

— ✺ —

Michael and I stayed in our relationship pattern for the next three years. We emailed, chatted online, talked on the phone about once a week, and saw each other in person as frequently as our schedules allowed.

During the warmer months, I went to powwows, and he continued to acknowledge me secretly over the loud speaker in ways that went unnoticed by his Indian friends. It wasn't uncommon for him to make off-the-wall comments, and the audience just assumed it was Michael's attempt at being funny. I merely smiled and shook my head, or nodded my head in agreement.

I loved playing the game even though I would have preferred throwing caution to the wind and kissing him for all the world to see. But the potential consequences kept me from mustering up the courage to do it. Instead, I ignored that inner inkling that something was off-center, and distracted myself by thinking about something else or eating to numb my feelings.

I enjoyed powwows. I loved watching the dancers, listening to the singers and the drumming. The sounds resonated deeply in my soul. As time passed, I became more and more familiar with the Denver Indian community, but I never interacted directly with any of them. They were friendly, in their way, usually greeting me with a smile or a head nod, but none of them engaged with me in conversation. I was not in a position to walk up and say, "Hi, you don't know me, but I know everything about you and your family. Don't worry, it's not likely your husband is going to lose his job when the funding for the position ends."

Sometimes, I wished I had the confidence to pretend I was a psychic reader. I could have made a small fortune at powwows. It would have blown their minds when I was able to tell them all I knew about their lives and their families. I probably could have retired even earlier!

My friends were kept up to date about my relationship with Michael. After some time had passed, they stopped asking me why I put up with his crap or when he was going to introduce me to his family and friends. They told me as long as I was willing to accept the situation, they wouldn't discourage me from loving him, not that they would have succeeded even if they'd tried. Most of them understood how deeply our private world absorbed me.

Smartphone technology was just beginning to emerge at that time, and being able to check my email on my BlackBerry became addictive. When I first heard the term "crack-berry," I actually laughed out loud and then groaned a little to myself because it was so true. The second summer that Michael and I were together, I hung out with my friend at an outdoor pool. It became a joke between us about how often I would find excuses to get out of the pool to check my phone. Finally one day, my friend brought a Ziplock bag to the pool, so I could keep the phone closer to the water and not worry about ruining it. Years later we still laugh about my addiction.

After Michael and I had dated for a few years, one of my co-workers decided to write a romance novel about a Native American man and a white woman who fell in love. The story's setting was in Montana, and three of us from the office decided to take a road trip up to the area where she was basing her book. At first, when I told Michael about the trip and subsequent book, he was very leery of the idea. When he saw she was serious, and that the book didn't have anything to do with him, he warmed up to the idea and even offered to answer research questions for her.

I was surprised when he told me I could pass her questions on to him, and he would answer them. I think she was even more surprised than I was, but gladly welcomed his information. For the next few months, I ran ideas past him. I never gave her Michael's direct contact information because I wanted to stay in the loop. Technically, I was proofreading everything she wrote, so it just seemed to make sense that I would serve as a conduit. I didn't see this at the time, but it was a way I could maintain some sense of control over their interactions.

About the same time the book was finished, Michael wanted to sponsor an Otoe-Missouria Tail Dance in Denver. The Tail Dance is a traditional dance of his tribe down in Oklahoma. He was excited by the idea of being able to sponsor the event, but he couldn't afford the down payment to rent the Denver Indian Center. He explained to me how important the dance was to his people, and he felt like he was letting his tribe down because he couldn't arrange for the dance. Without a second thought, I asked, "How much do you need to reserve the Indian Center?"

He was quiet and said, "Five hundred dollars, but I only have a hundred."

Taking his hand I said, "Don't worry about it, I can cover the other four. I can see how important this is to you."

His first response was, "I can't let you do that."

I told him he didn't have a choice and the next day, I went to the bank, withdrew the money, and dropped it off to him at his office.

It took a few weeks for him to arrange for the Tail Dance. Once he had the Denver Indian Center reserved, he told me I could invite my writer friend from work to attend the event with me. Wow! A first! He had actually invited me to go the Denver Indian Center for the event. Prior to that dance, he hadn't forbidden me from going to events; he just had never formally invited me. I was excited to go, and had a secret hope he would openly acknowledge me since he told me to bring a friend.

The Tail Dance, more formally known as an *E'loska* or War Dance, is a ceremonial dance originally associated with celebrating the war journey. The *E'loska* dance style is considered a straight dance, in contrast to the exhibition style of powwow dancing. The ceremony dance flows with simple grace and dignity using just a basic dance step. At the middle of the song, the dancers look about as if trying to find the trail of an enemy in past time. In a more contemporary sense, the dancers are searching for their direction and guidance in life for a path of success. As the song continues, the dancer resumes a more upright stance, having found his direction, to continue on and pursue success.

Looking back at the *E'loska*, I realize it was a great metaphor for what was happening on my personal journey. Similar to the dancers searching for their guidance, I, too, had been searching for my answers.

It didn't dawn on me at that point I was attempting to buy my way into his world. There was no material boundary I wasn't willing to cross to keep this man in my life. Somehow none of it mattered because I was in love, and somewhere in my brain I still believed he would change his mind and openly announce that he loved me.

I justified in my mind his inviting me to the event was a sure sign I was beginning to break down his cultural barriers. I believed there was still a good chance he would openly love me because he kept telling me he couldn't imagine his life without me in it. I was still willing to accept being invisible in Michael's Native world, because I knew it was just a matter of time, and he would announce how he loved me to the Indian world.

I had mixed feelings while we were at the Indian Center. I realized that only one of the reasons Michael was comfortable inviting me was because I had my friend from work with me.

It was also that night I was shocked to realize he'd also invited another woman there. In time, I came to know her as his Indian "beard." At least that's how he justified her existence in his life.

There I sat in the middle of the Denver Indian Center, face-to-face with the woman everyone else there thought he was dating. There was nothing I could do but smile and pretend I wasn't bothered by her presence. It helped that I was very excited, because Michael was finally allowing me to enter into the community in a small way. Seeing her sitting there, I was also suddenly aware of some of the consequences of his lies. I doubted she had any idea what was happening. I had never been "the other woman," and I found myself facing my insecurities and feelings of unworthiness because I knew about her. I hated knowing he was living a lie with me, while everyone else in his world believed something else.

The next day when I confronted him about her, he told me he needed to be interested in an Indian woman so the Native American community would not be concerned about him still being single. He told me he picked a woman who lived out of town so she wouldn't interfere in my relationship with him. He hadn't told me because he knew I would be upset about it. It was challenging for me to accept he was using that woman as his cover. I *was* upset and, although it was uncomfortable, it was just one more thing I was still willing to tolerate because I didn't want to lose him.

CHAPTER 14

— ♪ —

As my day-to-day life continued, I remained happily in denial and hid from the actual drudgery of my life by focusing on my love for Michael. I felt totally loved and embraced by him when we were alone.

It didn't dawn on me I was continually attempting to push/buy my way into his world. For example, at Christmas I gave Michael $500 in merchant gift cards. Michael in turn, would give them to Lance as an anonymous donation from someone at work. Lance would pass them out to some of the Denver Indian community elders. The elders used the gift cards to buy gifts for their grandchildren for Christmas. It was like multi-level gift giving, and I felt a great deal of pride in being able to make at least two generations of people very happy. Surely that kind of generosity would get Michael's attention and he would eventually want to tell Lance that the "anonymous" donor was actually the love of his life.

As time passed, though, my magical thinking stopped working and I began to acknowledge a feeling that something was terribly askew. Through therapy, I slowly began to sense a possible connection between the roles I had taken on while trying to please my parents and my willingness to please Michael by staying silent and invisible in our relationship.

I had moments in which I wondered if I had lost all sense of myself. Continuing to be unseen in Michael's world bothered me, but I just wasn't willing to make waves and risk losing him. In an odd way, it seemed to parallel my situation at work where I was also feeling unseen and unaccepted professionally. I hated to acknowledge my fear of making waves at work. I had worked too hard to please the new administration and—although things had started to change drastically at that point—heeding my father's advice, I still did not want to get caught on the wrong side of the political forces at work.

Thankfully by this time Michael and I no longer emailed as much, and it was easier for me to concentrate on my job. I managed to ride the fence fairly successfully for the first few years of the new administration, but I could sense the political horizon was changing even more.

My willingness to go along to get along was no longer effective in my work environment because their fear out-maneuvered my ability to keep up with the changing tides. Eventually one day I went into work and learned they were moving my office down to the second floor, away from the power center of the third floor. Shortly after I moved offices they promoted my boss. A new captain was appointed to oversee our area. He was a few years younger than I was. I was a forty-five-year-old, very large woman trying to be invisible, or at least not make waves. Actively following my weird attempt to hide and stay out of the way, there he was, younger, trying to be bigger. It's no wonder we never saw the world through the same lenses.

In our first official meeting, he told me he had been asking around, and so far no one could explain to him what I did. He proceeded to give me three days to prepare a document to validate my position within the agency. I was told to justify the specifics of why accreditation was important and, very sarcastically, he added, "Don't bother saying 'Because the sheriff said so.'"

At that moment, I sensed my professional life was changing, yet I still believed my years of collaboration and loyalty to the sheriff would protect me because I knew accreditation was important to him. I would jump through hoops for my new supervisor and play his game. Within the allotted amount of time, I put together the document. It described why accreditation was important, not only to our agency, but to every law enforcement agency in the country. There was no way he could argue with my points because, despite his remark, the underlying message in my report was, "The sheriff thinks so, too."

After I jumped through his hoops, he did pay lip service to me, but there was still unrest in the political environment. I couldn't quite put my finger on it, but something was amiss.

About that same time I became aware of a hidden camera that had been placed directly outside of my office, recording my every action. I remain forever grateful to being tipped off, and, although it no longer matters, my source will always stay anonymous. As I processed my feelings of betrayal, I was tempted to go in and throw a complete hissy fit, but I realized my best course of action was not to let on to anyone that I knew the camera was there.

I pretended I wasn't aware of the camera for the next two weeks and pretty much went on about my daily business. To an overweight, body-shame-based woman, the thought of being on camera was the worst kind of torture. It was also a major sign my career had dipped to an all-time low, and I was obviously not being trusted to do my job. I knew the administration was paranoid, but secret surveillance was beyond anything I would ever have dreamed they would do to me. It was one of the lowest points of both my personal and my professional life. However, I had written the policy, and I knew the agency had the authority to monitor activity in any way they felt was necessary.

During the time the camera was on, I also had a twenty-minute visit from the Human Resources Manager to do a "job study" of my position. I had been told the administration was doing a job audit on my position at the request of my boss. It was at that point the pieces of the puzzle slowly fell into place. They were looking for a way to either get rid of me or get rid of my position.

Ironically, because they didn't know I was aware of their plan, I gathered my wits about me and had two of the most productive weeks of my career. There was no way they could prove I wasn't working hard, and I made damn sure there wasn't a moment of down time during my day. It wasn't a lot different from my normal day-to-day activities because I didn't want to tip them off that

I was aware of their game, but I made sure I was extra intentional of the actions I performed while I was in my office.

As a result, no changes were made in my position or my responsibilities right away. If it had been a legitimate job study, they should have actually given me a substantial raise for the amount of work I accomplished while they watched. I kept waiting to be told they decided I didn't do enough work, and I was going to throw it back in their faces, but it never came to that. Whoever observed my activities on the other side of the camera must have been objective enough to report I was working my ass off.

CHAPTER 15

— ♫ —

Between having a new boss and realizing I teetered toward an assignment change, my stress level spilled over the top. Dating Michael added to the chaos of my life, more than he distracted me from it. I had begun to acknowledge how dysfunctional our relationship was. In addition, I was dealing with settling my dad's estate, even though it had been four years since he had died. I knew something in my life needed to change because I felt as if I were about to implode.

Along with my stress level, my weight skyrocketed, and I felt as if I were losing my mind. Part of me knew that Michael and I would never be able to find a long-term solution because of his beliefs about the Native American community. I was still unwilling to upset him and cause him to end our relationship. When times were good between us, it was pure heaven, and when he wouldn't open up his world to me, I was beyond frustrated.

I could not imagine my life without him, but I knew I didn't want to continue in the same way for much longer. I had spent precious years playing the game with him, and although I wanted more, and he knew it, he was completely unwilling to change anything. I didn't bring the topic up very frequently because he would just shut down. Every few months, though, I would broach the subject of meeting Lance or his drum group, or pretty much any damn Indian in his circle.

That December, Michael had been scheduled to emcee a powwow down in Colorado Springs, and I had gone to watch and then take him to tour the decorations of the Broadmoor Hotel afterward. I would have loved to surprise him with dinner at the Broadmoor, but they required reservations. There simply was no way to know what time he would finish at the powwow. I just planned to stop at one of their bars and have a few drinks and then go somewhere else for dinner.

He didn't know about my plan. I told him when the powwow was over that I would meet him at the Starbucks near I-25 and Circle Avenue. I picked that location because it was far enough away from the powwow, and I knew he would not worry about being seen with me. It was also close enough to the Broadmoor so I could find my way there. When he arrived, I asked him if I could drive, and he left his truck in the parking lot. We were talking about one of his friends at the powwow as I drove up to street to the Broadmoor, and he stopped and asked me where I was going. I told him I wanted to show him how beautifully decorated the hotel was for the holiday. He said, "Cool."

We drove up to the hotel, and I realized there was a large event, and we weren't going to be able to park easily and get a drink. He said, "That's fine. I'm tired. Let's just drive around and then go get dinner somewhere."

As we drove around the perimeter of the hotel, I was surprised to see there weren't more lights and decorations. As we made the last of the loop around the property, I said to Michael, "I thought there would be more."

He looked at me and said, "Of course you did. You always want more."

He said it in such a way I knew he was talking about something beyond the Christmas decorations. I turned it into a joke, laughed, and said, "Yes, I will always want more."

Yet deep inside I wondered, *Would I ever get more from Michael?*

We immediately left the Broadmoor, and I drove Michael back to his truck and followed him to an inexpensive family-style restaurant on the other side of town. Once again, I knew he picked the restaurant because he didn't want to risk any of his Indian friends seeing him with me.

After that trip I started to realize I needed some professional support. His comment plagued me between Christmas and the New Year. We had a nice Christmas Eve together, but he had to work on New Year's Eve, and I found myself sitting home watching the Dick Clark Special alone. The following week, I pulled out the business card of a Psychologist a friend of mine had told me about. I made my first appointment with her.

In my first session with Jude, we spent the entire hour merely getting background information. My biggest issue was my fear around anyone I worked with finding out that I was in therapy. Although my health insurance would have covered at least a portion of the expenses to see her, I chose to pay cash so there would not be an insurance paper trail. Although it cost me a lot more money to pay cash for therapy, I felt safer knowing no one could use the information against me.

My therapist Jude became very familiar with my world. Looking back, I realize if I'd actually had deeper friendships, they would have been less-expensive sounding boards, but at that time I wasn't willing or able to be vulnerable with my friends.

It was likely because of the way my position at work had been classified that I didn't have many actual peers. I longed for better friends, yet I see why I never really connected with other women at work. I was either in a position above them, in which I judged their work product, or I felt inferior to them because of my weight. I had grown up feeling like I was not socially acceptable because of the size of my body. It was a lonely, exclusionary existence.

When things were good between Michael and me, the loneliness wasn't a big deal, but as I realized Michael might never change his mind about openly dating me, I plummeted deeper into loneliness.

After a few weeks of sessions, my therapist asked me to consider seeing her twice a week. She came right out and told me she was worried about the stress I was under, and she knew I needed a place where I could begin to identify and dissect my feelings.

In those first several weeks we talked about my family and how they had raised me. She tried to get me to see patterns I had established as survival mechanisms. She suggested it might be in my best interest to take a deeper look at the dynamics of my family.

It didn't take long before she questioned me about some of my recent choices, including buying a house within a half-mile of Michael's apartment. She wondered if I made a calculated move to either convince him to move in with me or for me to keep a closer eye on him. The suggestion offended me at the time. I thought I'd bought the house because it was the perfect fit for me. It had the right layout. It was a ranch style patio home I thought I could grow old in. I defended my decision with such ferocity she looked at me and said, "I think thou protests too much."

My response was to burst into tears and admit she was probably right on both counts. I hoped Michael would change his mind and marry me, and we would grow old together in the house. In the meantime, I was close enough for midnight booty calls, and it was less of a concern for either one of us to drink and drive because I was within walking distance. Thankfully, she was able to convince me not to ask him to move in with me, at least until after he was ready to bring me openly into his world. She knew I was considering using the house as a leveraging piece to motivate him to let his friends and family know about me.

One of the greatest benefits of therapy was having the added protection of doctor–patient confidentiality. I could share with Jude all of the insanity around me at work. She helped me to decipher some of the events that occurred with the new administration. Although I found it difficult to begin with, she got me to see that the new sheriff may not have been who or what he seemed.

It was nice to have a place where I could openly discuss issues I didn't dare discuss with anyone inside or outside of the agency. I had unintentionally landed on the wrong side of the political fence, and there was no longer anyone inside the agency protecting me. There were political arrows flying every week, and most everyone around me just did their best to either duck or push someone else out in front them to take the hit. I was in a precarious position, and neither my therapist nor I could figure out exactly what I could do to get back on top.

I felt as if I were walking on eggshells both at work and with Michael. Although I could not see a light at the end of either one of those tunnels, I did my best to not give up hope.

Therapy probably kept me from caving in on myself. The political environment at work was tenuous even on the best days. "Leadership by fear" had become deeply embedded in the new management style. There had always been a little fear attached to keeping the previous sheriff happy, but there was a deeper, more profound level of fear-mongering in the new administration. It seeped its way down from the top, and, as a result, morale in the entire agency dipped.

The light-hearted office environment we experienced as an agency in the '90s had completely disappeared. My stress levels continued to escalate. It didn't help matters that people never accepted or liked the job tasks I was required to do. I couldn't separate them not liking the assignment

I was doing from them not liking me personally. It took a great emotional toll on me every time someone made a negative comment about accreditation. I knew it was human nature to not want to have someone critique your work product, but personally, it was hell to walk into an area for inspection and have everyone groan at my arrival. I took their negativity to heart.

The distraction provided by my, albeit unhealthy, relationship with Michael was nevertheless my escape. I loved the time we spent together. Although I kept hoping against hope that he would change his mind and publicly proclaim his love for me, I took the love he did offer and ran with it for as long as I could.

CHAPTER 16

— ♪♪ —

Michael's favorite musical artist was George Strait. He mentioned George Strait or referred to his music dozens of times when he emceed powwows. I overheard people calling Michael the "Indian George Strait" on more than one occasion. One of the first CDs Michael burned for me was full of George Strait songs.

In yet another unconscious effort to buy Michael's love, for his birthday I bought tickets for him to see George Strait perform. As an extra special surprise, I got floor seats next to the aisle where the artists enter the stage. I knew no one else in his life could afford to spend the hundreds of dollars on concert tickets that would get him close to the man he considered a living legend.

The concert was a few weeks before his birthday. I planned to surprise him, but it was impossible to get him to agree to not make plans on a Saturday night without telling him why. A couple of weeks before the concert, I broke down and told him what I planned. He was surprised when I told him we had tickets to the concert and over-the-top thrilled when I told him the location of the seats.

I secretly hoped the concert tickets would finally be

the catalyst that fueled his desire to show the world openly that he loved me.

During one of our conversations, he told me he planned to have a party at his house after the concert. Although he never actually invited me to the party, somehow I made the assumption it would ultimately be the night I got to meet his friends and family.

On the night of the concert, he picked me up, and we went to dinner at a steakhouse almost twenty miles away from the concert venue. I couldn't imagine why he picked a restaurant so far away, but my excitement kept me from focusing on what his motive might be. We had a nice dinner and drove downtown to the arena. During the drive, I noticed Michael was a little on edge, but I didn't give it a lot of thought at first.

While we were sitting there, waiting for the pre-concert show to start, Michael's cell phone rang. Because of the noise I couldn't tell exactly what he said, but I was pretty sure I heard him say, "I wish you were here, too." Again, I didn't give it a lot of thought. I figured he was just expressing his excitement about being in some of the best seats for the show. Once the concert started, Michael started to relax and enjoy himself.

Between the opening act and the main concert, Michael went up to the concourse to go to the bathroom and came back with two bags of souvenirs. He gave me a huge thermos cup and a towel and told me the rest of the gifts were for Bubba and the boys. George Strait was a tremendous performer, and the concert was amazing. As he left the stage, before his encore, he stopped and shook

Michael's hand. Michael said to him, "Thank you for everything you have done. You've always been my hero."

Looking Michael in the eye George said, "Thank you. It's been my honor."

As we turned around, Michael said, "Oh what the f—," took me in his arms and kissed me passionately. He took me by the hand and said, "I don't care who in the f— sees us. I have never been happier in my life."

He smiled brilliantly and added, "Lady, you rock!"

He was beaming from meeting George Strait, and I beamed because he had showered me with love in a public display of affection.

After the encore, we made our way back to his truck. It was after midnight by the time we pulled out of the parking lot. When Michael realized what time it was, he asked me how much beer I had at home, he pointed to the clock and said that the liquor stores had closed. Apparently he hadn't had time before the concert to stock up for the party. I told him I had two cases in the fridge at home, and he was welcome to stop by my house and pick up it before we went back to his house. He didn't respond, but just started heading to my house. We talked about the concert the whole way home. Michael kept saying how grateful he was for the evening. I knew it was the big shift I'd been waiting for.

We pulled up to my house, and after he had put the beer in his truck he turned to me and said, "Thanks for giving me one of the greatest nights of my life!"

"You're welcome, but the night is still young," I said playfully.

"Yes, I can't wait to tell the boys about what a great time I've had tonight. Thanks again. Goodnight."

I stood next to his truck completely dumbfounded. "Are you going home alone?"

He looked at me funny and said, "Yes, you know the boys are waiting for me."

In a blinding flash, reality hit me. Even after spending hundreds of dollars and going out of my way to make sure he had an incredible concert experience, I was still not going to get invited into his world.

He simply shrugged his shoulders, got back in his truck and pulled away. I was stunned, my heart shattered into a million pieces.

CHAPTER 17

— ✿ —

I stood in my driveway and watched him pull away, waiting for him to turn around and drive back. After a few minutes it dawned on me that he wasn't going to return and my emotions crashed in. I paced back and forth in my house, trying to figure out what to do next. I was beyond disappointed and upset. I was enraged—angry with him for leaving, and angry with myself for continuing to believe he was ever going to let me into his world. I could not figure out what steps to take next.

One part of me wanted to go over to his apartment and bang on the door and make a big scene. Truthfully, I was afraid to do something that radical, partly because I was afraid of the depth of my rage, but mainly because I was afraid one of his neighbors would call the police. With all of the latest drama I was afraid of potential repercussions at work. The last thing I needed to do was give them an actual reason to discipline me. I'm amazed that I had enough clear-headedness to figure that much out, as mad as I was. Part of me wanted to run away, to escape the pain I was feeling. The thought of living my life without him was more painful than I could fathom.

My heart and mind played tug-o-war. I pondered whether or not he could change, and whether or not I could continue to pretend I didn't care that he wouldn't. I paced. I cried. Then I paced and stomped my feet, screaming and cussing with every footstep. I continued to pace and pace and pace until, finally, I flopped down on my bed, exhausted.

I felt like a caged animal trapped in our relationship without a way to escape. Every option seemed impossible or too painful to endure. I didn't have any experience expressing anger. I hadn't yet learned healthy forms of release, and my history had always been to turn anger inward or to numb it with food.

I kept replaying the events of the concert in my head. How could Michael publicly take me in his arms and kiss me passionately one minute, then casually drop me off at my house and remind me I would never be good enough? Would he ever change? Could he ever change? How long was I willing to wait? How much more time and money was I willing to spend?

I played the concert through in my mind for the hundredth time. I reflected back on all of the things I had done over the last few years trying to get Michael to bring me into his world. I looked at not only the money I had spent, but—more importantly—the times I had stayed invisible, wholly in the name of earning his love.

What more could I do? How much more was I willing to take? What if he never changed his mind?

Agonizingly I accepted that he was NEVER going to change his mind. Michael would not ever be capable of openly loving me in a manner that felt acceptable to me. I hated to admit it to myself. It was time to face that no matter what I did or didn't do, no matter how deeply I wished for it, Michael was never going to acknowledge our relationship to his friends and family. My best attempts at earning or buying his love had failed.

As the reality dawned, my thoughts started down an even darker path. Had any man ever really loved me? Yes, I'd been with other men before Michael, but none of them ever made me feel the way Michael did when we were alone. My thoughts even went all the way back to my childhood, and I wondered if my dad had ever been able to love me as a daughter.

The more I considered my history, the angrier I became; and the angrier I became, the more I turned it in on myself. I began to wonder if I could or would ever really be loved. Even words from my childhood haunted me—my mom telling me, "No one will ever love a fat girl."

There were times, I knew, when my mom had difficulty loving and accepting me. Maybe my mom was right; maybe my fat did make me unlovable. That thought made me even angrier. I danced between directing my anger to the people of my past and directing the anger inward to myself. Turning my fury inside, I wondered *would I ever be loveable*? I felt hopeless, as though there were no way out of the darkness. All of the stress of my entire life spiraled into the depths of my core, and I wondered if there was any reason to continue trying to live. It was one of the darkest nights of my life.

Thankfully my friend Kelly was a night owl, and I

knew I could reach out and call her, even at 2:00 a.m. to vent. With deep gulping sobs I explained what was going on, and she just let me cry. She encouraged me to scream and get the feelings out. Most of all, for a couple of hours, she held the space for me to find for myself that there was a way out. She gently reminded me that I was a great person. She listed every positive thing she could think of that I had accomplished. She told me repeatedly I deserved better than Michael's treatment.

It took a couple of hours, but it started to sink in, and I began to accept what I needed to do. I made the decision to end the relationship. It was a long, hard, brutal winding road to get to that decision. The more I replayed the history between Michael and me, the more it sank in that Michael would never be willing to change.

Deep in my gut I also knew if I confronted him, he would just twist my words around on me and somehow make me wrong. I didn't have the courage to stand up to him. I knew I didn't have the coping skills to face him. The only way I would be able to pull off breaking up with him was to sever my ties completely using the same means of communication with which we had started. I sent him an email.

The email was short and sweet. I told him I was terribly hurt by not being invited back to his house to meet his friends and family. I said I would love him until the day I died, but I needed more than he would ever be willing to give me. I finally accepted he was not going to change, and, as a result, I no longer wanted to have anything to do with him.

I spent the next few days praying Michael would see the error of his ways. He'd show up on my doorstep with flowers and all of his Indian family and friends, and he'd proclaim his love for me.

Instead he emailed me back and simply said, "Whatever you want." I'm pretty sure he didn't believe I was serious.

To that point, his next emails seemed like nothing was wrong between us, he'd forward me jokes or stories like he'd been doing for years. He even tried to call, but didn't leave a message. Slowly, his emails decreased in frequency, and he never took responsibility for what he'd done. I was proud of myself for not responding to him.

As days turned into weeks, his words became harsh. In several of his emails, he told me he didn't have the time or energy to spend on someone who didn't want to be with him. I held my ground.

I had spent years trying to get him to love me, and once I finally accepted the reality of the situation, I was no longer able to go back and pretend it would ever be anything different.

To fill the hole in my life, I dove back into work. I inadvertently started a new daily routine. Every morning I got a large coffee on the way to the office; otherwise, I skipped breakfast. Around lunchtime I would go to one of the popular fast food drive-thrus near the office. I always ordered enough food to appear as if I were ordering for two people, pretending that I was taking lunch back to a friend.

I would find a parking lot and inhale both lunches knowing once the food settled in, my kaleidoscope of feelings would numb. Most afternoons, I would get so sleepy I would have to drink a couple of diet sodas to get enough caffeine to stay awake during my food coma. As soon as I got off work, I would do the drive-thru at yet another fast food restaurant on the way home. A couple of times a week, I went to the liquor store and stocked up on my favorite kind of beer. On those nights, I went home to eat and drink until I passed out on the couch. In the middle of the night, I woke up long enough to drag myself to bed.

I am not sure how I always managed to get up and get back to work on time the next day, but I always did. Each morning I vowed to stop this decimating pattern, but continued to follow the same routine for months. Besides therapy, it was the only thing I knew to help lower my stress levels and cope with the breakup. On some level, I knew it was probably hurting me, but truthfully, I no longer cared. By that point even my therapist was frustrated by trying to help me, but I have no doubt the twice-weekly appointments were my only saving grace.

The more I followed that destructive routine, the more isolated and lonely my life became. Over the years I had decreased my circle of friends so I would be available at the drop of the hat for Michael, and once he was no longer in my life, my circle felt empty.

Instead of doing something to increase the size of my group of friends, I increased the size of my body in an unconscious effort to keep people even further away. It was not a conscious effort to get bigger, or even to isolate or withdraw, but it was very effective in creating a cocoon of isolation. As time moved on, I became more detached and cared about myself less.

Michael still tried to contact me, on occasion, usually sending me innocuous information about his job or the Native community. Sporadically, he would leave a drunken message on my voicemail. He said he missed talking to me, but mostly rambled on about what was going on with him. I usually ignored his calls, but occasionally answered to see if he had anything new to say. He rarely did. The calls become less frequent, and my life continued its lonely, slow spiral deeper into hell.

CHAPTER 18

— ♫ —

Eventually I stopped all self-care. I no longer gave a damn about anything. I had no incentive to shave my legs, or put on a nice-smelling lotion. There was no need to prepare my body to share it with someone else anymore. I didn't realize it at the time, but because my body was getting bigger, it was more and more difficult to keep myself clean, and I often had an odor. People tried in subtle ways to let me know, but no one had the nerve—or cared enough about me—to speak to me openly about how offensively I smelled. It takes a good friend to tell you when you have hygiene issues, and I no longer had anyone close enough to say anything. My therapist never brought it to my attention; or if she tried, it was never in a way that could penetrate my psyche.

I stopped buying new clothes. There had been a time when I was younger that I put a lot of thought and effort into my wardrobe, but it was no longer important. The more weight I gained, the more anesthetized I became to my inner pain. The pain's intensity caused me to push the outside world further away. Taking care of my physical body was no longer a priority.

My unconscious top priority was to hide from the world in general and to keep my emotional pain at bay. Using my weight as armor, I built thick walls around me that no one dared to infiltrate. I wanted to be invisible in the world, and I already knew being overweight kept me from being seen, so instinctively I dug that hole a little deeper.

If it hadn't been for my therapist, my life could easily have been destroyed. I hung on to those two hours of therapy every week as a lifeline. Without Jude's support, I would not have survived.

My medical doctor was concerned about the amount of weight I was gaining and suggested at one point that I see a nutritionist; however, my emotional pain and my mind's denial of the size of my body kept me from following any nutrition plan for more than a few days. I could not bear to live my life without excess food and alcohol; they were the only means I had to diminish the pain.

I was isolated and numb, and I didn't have the energy to do anything more than the minimal amount of work needed to keep a paycheck coming in. The more my personal life spiraled out of control, the deeper my professional life plummeted. I didn't have the energy to perform at the same level. I was no longer at the peak of my career. Working a twelve-hour day no longer existed as a possibility in my world. I was lucky to get in the scheduled nine-and-a-half hours. My immune system became compromised; my sick leave use increased as I caught every virus and bug floating around the office.

Fortunately, over the years I had accumulated well over

400 hours of leave, so my supervisors couldn't challenge my sick-leave use. I helped draft the sick-leave policy, so I also knew how to get around it. I was ill during the last three days or the first three days of my workweek, just long enough to fall below the point where my supervisor could ask for a doctor's note. The one time I was off work and sick for two weeks, the bosses made me fill out FMLA paperwork, but my doctor gave me a note with no issue. I was pissed because they had never needed documentation from me before, and I felt like I was being picked on, but, in the end, I jumped through their hoops and shrugged it off.

To add to the stress, I had yet another new boss. The political environment was in more turmoil, and fear had escalated to an all-time high. My new supervisor was even more demanding than the last. Part of me understood he was just doing what he had to do to fit the role they assigned to him. My career was in the middle of a long, slow, skid out of control.

It was a sad day when I realized my new boss might not be willing to hold the other commanders accountable to compliance with accreditation standards. I had a sick feeling in the pit of my stomach that our upcoming audit wasn't going to go as well as the ones we'd had in the past, but by that time, my give-a-damn meter was already damaged. It finally sank in—there wasn't anything I could do to change the political environment, and although I had been ignoring the handwriting on the wall, it was coming into focus, and it was scary. I had to admit that my dad had been right after all.

The change in bosses, including the changes in political environment and my sub-par energy level, meant I no longer had any desire to even attempt to follow the winds of change. I just prayed I could hang on to our agency's old reputation with the incoming audit team. If we got the right team in to inspect us, everything would be okay. If not, God only knew what would happen.

Sure enough, the inspection team was selected, and almost immediately, I knew we were in for trouble. CALEA had just implemented a new reporting system, and the team leader began making demands weeks before the team ever arrived on site in August. A small group of us scrambled for two weeks to create the report they requested. When we submitted the report, the team leader rejected the majority of the data. I'd never had an official report rejected prior to that one.

My boss sensed the process was not going to go well, and his only excuse was that he had never been involved with accreditation before. He kept pleading innocence and ignorance to the big boss. I could sense a bus about to run me over, but what I didn't anticipate was the velocity of its impact.

When the assessment team arrived on site, my boss decided it would be better if he picked up the team leader at the airport. In the twenty years I had been managing accreditation, I never had anyone else be the first contact with the team, but this time I did not have a choice. I don't know what my boss said to the team leader, or if it could have made a difference had I been there myself.

I liked working with the other two team members, and

at one point, I held out hope they would be able to calm the leader down, but that never happened. The inspection team let us know there was no way we would be getting the perfect score we were seeking. I doubted anyone else would be held responsible for not achieving perfection.

Thankfully I already had approval to take six weeks' vacation immediately after the inspection. My co-workers knew I planned to use my vacation and take a trip to Sedona, Arizona to buy an investment home. I planned to use it as a winter home for retirement three years later. I just needed to hang on a few more years, and I would be free to retreat completely from my work life and get as far away from the insanity as possible.

CHAPTER 19

—— ✦ ——

The week following the inspection was a tough one. I knew we did not get the result everyone assumed we would get. It was the first time an inspection team left our agency that I did not feel proud of my role. Part of the issue was not feeling well physically; but more than that, I wondered if there were going to be repercussions for not getting the perfect score.

The sheriff was kind, and seemed to take the identified issues in stride, but I feared and doubted his words. I was embarrassed, and I knew he was as well. The inspection had been the roughest I'd ever participated in, on either side of the table.

I had never been on the receiving end of a non-compliance issue during any of our previous inspections and didn't have a clear idea how to react. Based on our agency's past performance, I believed the Team Leader had held us to an unreasonable interpretation of the standard, but there was nothing we could do about it until the final report was written and submitted in a few weeks.

CHAPTER 20

— ♪♪ —

I was distraught and overwhelmed when I began my vacation the following week, both physically and emotionally exhausted. I was grateful I didn't have to interact with anyone from the agency until the middle of October. I planned to take a few days to rest up and get ready to hit the road, but even after a couple of days of rest, I felt worse. The amount of stress I had been under over the summer had compromised my immune system. I just couldn't quite seem to shake the bronchitis or whatever made me so short of breath. I called, and thankfully my doctor had an opening that day, September 1, 2009.

I was grateful he could see me right away. I knew that the sooner I could get diagnosed, the quicker I would feel better, and I could get on with my plans to head to Arizona and prepare for my future. I was tired of feeling sick and tired, but more than that, I just needed to escape.

When I got to the doctor's office, following their normal routine, they took me back to the "staging area." My temperature was 101.3°F, my blood pressure 195/110, and my oxygen level 82 (95 is considered normal at our altitude). The nurse was shocked to see my oxygen level so low, so she instructed me to drop my hands to my side and take several slow, deep breaths. After a minute of deep breathing she re-tested my oxygen level, and it had only risen to 85.

She took me to an exam room, found a portable oxygen tank, and got the doctor. After supplementing me on three liters of oxygen, they only raised my oxygen level to 93.

My doctor, surprised it hadn't risen higher, sent me with my oxygen tank across the hall to radiology for a chest x-ray. He instructed me to return to the exam room, and he asked radiology to read and report the results to him right away.

Ironically my only reaction at that point was to feel shame for needing to drag the oxygen tank with me. I was too emotionally detached from my body to understand that it actually helped me. I just knew everyone in the waiting room was looking at me and judging me for being another fat woman who never took care of herself.

Thankfully, the X-ray technician was very compassionate. She took an X-ray on one machine, and told me the machine wasn't functioning properly and suggested we try a machine in the next room. After the second X-ray on the larger machine, she sent me directly back to the exam room. She assured me someone would be over to talk with me shortly. Never once did she let on about what she saw. If I thought I would have been able to get by without it, I would have dumped the tank for the return trip across the hall and avoided the embarrassment of schlepping the stupid tank with me.

After a few minutes, my doctor came in, sat down,

and told me he was alarmed by the results of my X-ray. He was so concerned that he had gone over to radiology to read it himself. My heart was enlarged. He went on to say that he couldn't tell for sure what was going on, and he wanted me to go the emergency room. Whatever was happening appeared to be pretty serious. He said that he should probably send me by ambulance, but if I promised him I would go directly to the emergency room, he would let me drive myself and save $500 in ambulance costs.

Even with everything he'd said, I didn't think I was that sick, but I promised him I would go directly to the hospital. It was about a thirty-minute drive to the hospital that was covered by my insurance. I left his office once again with the stupid tank in tow, still feeling ashamed of it. Being concerned about WHY I needed to be on oxygen never occurred to me.

As I drove to the hospital, I realized I hadn't had lunch and decided to do the drive-thru at Arby's and pick up a sandwich to eat on my way. I had a feeling it would be a while before I could be seen and released, so figured I might as well make sure I had eaten something before I got there.

I was relieved to find the hospital had valet parking for the emergency room, so I left my car there and headed inside. The minute I told the woman at the counter my name, they rushed out with a wheelchair and hurried me back to an emergency room cubicle and hooked me up to a heart monitor and an EKG. During the flurry of activity they determined I had not had a heart attack, and things slowed down a bit. They had me do paperwork and pay the $300.00 emergency room fee. At least they determined I wasn't in immediate danger of dying before they collected my money.

After being poked and prodded by the attending physicians, the cardiologist on-call came in to introduce himself. While he examined me, he asked, "If your heart stops, do I have your permission to restart it?" His question flat stopped me in my tracks.

My initial response was, "No."

It wasn't that I had a conscious death wish, but the severity of the situation still had not sunk into my thick skull. I assumed he was talking about "end of life" care and I didn't understand I was actually in danger of dying.

Looking at me with complete indignation, "What do you mean 'No'? Do you have any idea what you're saying?"

I paused and considered the possibility of letting it all stop. Could I stop the insanity that had become my life? Was I ready to stop trying to force my round-peggedness into the square hole of the world around me?

In the end I said, "Yes, you can restart my heart."

Once he determined I didn't really mean "No," he asked me a dozen or so medical history questions. Since I didn't have a previous cardiac history on file, he said it would be up to him to determine what was happening.

They would be doing a chest CAT scan next and, depending on what they found, he would decide my course of treatment. As he explained the CAT scan to me, a technician rushed in to wheel me down to radiology.

The scan didn't take long, and I was relieved it wasn't

a full body scan like an MRI. As soon as the test was over, they wheeled me back to the ER and told me to rest until they got the results.

While I waited, I debated about whom I should notify that I was in the hospital. With the paperwork, I had listed my friend Kay as my emergency contact because the only immediate family I had was my sister, but she and I had not been in close contact the last few years.

I decided I should probably call Kay and let her know what was happening, just in case someone from the hospital called her. As soon as I called, she offered to come to the hospital, but I told her to hold off. They hadn't determined what was wrong with me. I said I would let her know if I needed her. I believed there was a chance they would release me and let me go home.

Finally the cardiologist came in to give me the results of my CAT scan. It appeared I had a pericardial effusion—the sac around my heart was full of infected fluid and was beginning to strangle my heart. He said he might need to go in and drain the fluid with a needle, and I needed to sign consent papers before we continued.

CHAPTER 21

— ♪♪ —

Once the doctor had my permission to save my life, the wheels began to turn quickly. He explained the different options he would consider over the next few days, including surgery to drain the fluid. That idea was not at all appealing, and the severity of my situation began to dawn on me.

The next thing I knew, the ER staff came into my cubicle, put in a catheter, and wheeled me up to Intensive Care. They started me on several intravenous medications and continued to monitor my heart very closely.

It still took me a couple of hours to comprehend what was happening to me. Once my body had the chance to fight off the infection, my condition started to improve pretty quickly.

Before the next morning, it was determined my heart was very strong, and I was moved down one floor to a cardiac monitoring unit. When the cardiologist came in, he told me I was lucky. The amount of fluid I had in the sac around my heart could have easily killed a "normal sized" person. It was the first time I'd had a medical professional tell me my cardiovascular system was used to working harder than normal due to my size; my being overweight might have actually saved my life. He said my heart needed a rest from working so hard, and he highly recommended I start taking better care of myself.

He ended the conversation saying I probably would not be as lucky the next time if I continued down this path. When I asked him what caused the issue in the first place, he said he wasn't sure. He told me they would be running tests over the next few days to see if they could determine the cause.

While they ran the tests, I laid in the hospital bed and re-evaluated my life. I hated the idea, but it was time to start being honest with myself and make some changes.

The longer I stayed in the bed, the more aware I became of what was happening to me. The first couple of days, I slept a lot. On the third day, I started to feel that there was more to life than I had been allowing myself to live, and I strengthened my resolve to make significant changes.

One of the biggest transitions was being able to sense my body again. I knew I would feel better if I took a shower. I was horrified, embarrassed, and ashamed when it took two nurses to help me walk thirty feet to the shower, and that— even on oxygen—I was too weak to stand up by myself. Luckily, the shower had a handicap bench, so I could sit and rest once I got there. The nurses left me for about ten minutes sitting in the shower with hot water running over me, and it felt fabulous. They came back in and helped me wash my hair and get clean. It took almost two hours for the entire process, and by the time I got back to my hospital bed, I was exhausted and slept a couple of hours.

After that shower the implications of my health status began to sink in. Up until that point, I had been able to pretend I would just take a couple of days to heal, and I would jump right back into my normal life. That shower was an intense effort. I was becoming willing to embrace whatever it was going to take to heal from that event. I wanted to make sure I was never in the same boat again.

The next morning, my cardiologist came in and was happy to hear I had the will to strive to get better. He told me his office offered a lot of different support programs to cardiac patients, and he would happily get me started with them as soon as the hospital released me. In the meantime, he asked if I wanted to meet with the hospital nutritionist to go over diet recommendations. Although I wasn't thrilled with the idea, I agreed to see her.

My hesitation came because I didn't want to accept the label of cardiac patient. I had so much shame around the idea of being sick that having a cardiac label was more than I could bear. Denial had been my salvation for so long, but it was no longer working. Looking back I now see I was not quite ready to give it up, but I couldn't really be invisible when I was that sick.

The shame and denial kept me from letting anyone else know I was in the hospital. I hated admitting to myself, let alone anyone else, that my life was completely out of control.

Only Kay knew where I was, and up until that point, I didn't want her to come and visit me. I specifically asked her not to say anything to anyone, and although she didn't agree with keeping my secret, she respected my wishes.

Finally, on the third day, I asked Kay to come visit after she went to my house and picked up a few things, mainly toiletries and my phone charger.

When she brought the items, she told me that when she had arrived at my house, she was startled because the TV was on. At first, she was afraid someone else was in the house. She was surprised when she looked around and saw the house was dirty and the trash had started to smell. I apologized for the mess she found and explained to her that when I left for the doctor, I had every intention of being home within an hour. I had planned to clean everything up before I headed out of town.

Looking back, I realize I had been much sicker than I ever imagined. Ordinarily I would never have left my house looking like that, not even for an hour.

During her visit, Kay convinced me it was time for me to let some other people know what was going on. I promised her that once my phone recharged, I would let some of my old friends know, but I made her promise not to tell anyone associated with where I worked. In my blind stubbornness, I was not going to give anyone at the office the satisfaction of knowing what sad shape I was in.

Ironically, I found out later, the wife of one of the commanders was working in the cardiac unit that week, but I was so out of it, I didn't even recognize her.

There weren't many people for me to contact because, at that time, I was pretty much isolated from most of my friends. Thankfully, the people I called gave me support and offered to help in any way.

In an emotionally weakened moment, I actually called

Michael to tell him what was happening. We had not talked for a couple of months and, surprisingly, we had a decent conversation. He told me he was convinced my illness was caused by stress from the assholes I worked with, and he was glad I had not died because he would have had to avenge my death.

There was a time those words would have thrilled me, but this time they just seemed hollow. As we continued to talk I noticed the old familiar pull with him was gone. It was one of the first positive signs that I was starting to get ready to put significant changes in place in my life.

CHAPTER 22

— ♪♪ —

The next day I met with the hospital nutritionist, and she suggested I get the book *Eat Right for Your Type*. She believed in the theory behind the book and believed it would be a good place for me to start. It all sounded good. I didn't know if I was ready to face the world without food as a crutch, but I promised her I would get the book. She also talked about needing a support structure in place, and I told her I'd previously attended a 12-Step group for overeating. She recommended I get back in touch with that group. She was kind and told me that, the way she saw it, I could take the event as a wake-up call and begin to make changes in my life, or I could ignore it. She didn't come right out and say it as directly as my cardiologist had, but she implied that if I didn't make some changes, I probably would not be as lucky the next time.

Finally, I was released from the hospital. I was upset because I still needed supplemental oxygen and had to arrange to have an oxygen condenser delivered to my house. My discharge papers said to limit my daily activity to no more than twenty minutes at a time on my feet and not to lift anything over ten pounds. I was only supposed to drive to and from doctor's appointments.

On the day I was released, Kay came to the hospital and drove me home. We stopped at the grocery store on the way, and she suggested I use one of the handicapped carts. I was beyond ashamed and told her, "No way in hell."

I walked about ten feet towards the store, and reluctantly I accepted I would need to use the cart. It was a humiliating experience for me. It didn't dawn on me until months later that it was not only okay to need the assistance, but to be grateful that the assistance was there. At the time though, I was too busy being embarrassed to be grateful.

The shame I felt about being sick in the first place was still overwhelming. I despised that being sick interfered with my denial system. I couldn't pretend to be healthy in my head while I dragged that damn oxygen tank everywhere I went. I was hell-bent on doing whatever it took to get off the oxygen. I knew that my life needed to change, but I refused to be seen as weak. It was hard to admit that I had such deep resentment of my physical condition. That resentment carried over to a terribly judgmental attitude about me needing assistance. More than anything I hated admitting I needed support; it's impossible to ask for help and stay invisible.

Ironically, I thought it was great that the assistance was available for people who needed it, but I stubbornly thought I was never going to be one of those people if I could help it. It took me several weeks of being humbled to get past some of those old, outdated beliefs. As the reality of my condition settled into my consciousness, I began to take advantage of the assistance available to me.

My primary care physician was pleased with the progress I'd made by the end of that first week, and I expressed to him my gratitude for how he'd handled the situation when I showed up at his office on death's doorstep.

The next visit, a couple of days later, my cardiologist ran some tests—the most significant being an echocardiogram—and was able to determine that my fluid had decreased by more than half in less than two weeks. He introduced me to his support staff and asked them to explain some of the post-care programs they offered.

One of the resources was working directly with an exercise physiologist to determine how soon I could start an exercise program. Another resource was counseling and post-cardiac life-skill lessons. I was impressed by how dedicated his staff was to the philosophy of making healthy lifestyle changes in a supportive atmosphere. I immediately signed up with the cardiac counselor.

My first appointment with the exercise physiologist was weeks later when I had built up some stamina on my own. In our first consultation he proposed thirty-minute sessions twice a week using the same treadmills and equipment used to do cardiac stress testing. I hated wheeling my oxygen tank into the medical building for the first appointment. Even more, I hated not being able to just jump on the treadmill and take it to the level I had been at just a couple of years before. I had not been athletic in any sense of the word, but I could walk and talk at the same time at a speed of three miles per hour.

During the first day of testing, the fastest he would set the treadmill was .5 miles per hour, and the worst part of it was how winded I became. Within ten minutes, I had to stop. Even with extra oxygen supplementation, I could not go any longer. I was so embarrassed that I just sat down next to the treadmill and bawled.

He told me to not be embarrassed. Many people who'd experienced a cardiac event needed to start very slowly.

I told him he didn't understand that I wasn't like regular cardiac people, whatever that meant.

He looked at me with great compassion and suggested I call my therapist and talk to her about all of the feelings that were coming up.

In addition to my therapist, the cardiac counselor was also a very compassionate woman and helped me start to see how I preferred to numb myself from the reality of my feelings. She suggested I order Cheryl Richardson's book *The Art of Extreme Self-Care* and begin to follow its guidelines. Those included beginning to do things that were comforting to my body besides food. Some of her favorite suggestions were taking a hot bath followed by putting a nice-smelling lotion all over my body, and sitting down with a cup of tea while journaling all of my feelings each day. During this time I also started doing mirror work using Louise Hay's affirmations.

Every morning after my shower, I stood in front of my huge bathroom mirror and said, "I love you. I accept you exactly as you are at this moment. I am loved, and I am lovable."

I felt my body slowly awaken. I was finally motivated to have a solid foundation of self-care in place.

I also got into the habit of watching humorous and uplifting things on TV while I rested. One of my favorite things to watch was my all-time favorite movie, *Last Holiday* with Queen Latifah. There is a scene in the movie where she's looking into the mirror. She thinks she's dying and says, "Next time... we will laugh more, we'll love more, we just won't be so afraid." The first time I watched that scene I cried because I felt the depth of my own sorrow and how I allowed fear to rule my life.

Happily, the next few exercise appointments went better. Each time, I was able to walk a little farther and a little faster. Between appointments, I walked on my treadmill at home. The more I progressed, the less oxygen I needed as well. After a couple of weeks, the exercise physiologist told me I could attempt to walk outside on my own. He asked me to carry the small portable tank with me the first few times just in case I needed it. If I continued making progress, I might be able to wean myself off the oxygen completely.

The first time I walked outside was a month to the day from when I had driven to the hospital. I drove to Washington Park, where they have a great flat path to walk around the lake. The trail is less than a mile, and I knew they also had benches along the path.

The first time I headed out to walk, I had my oxygen tank with me. I parked in the northwest parking lot and managed to walk about a hundred feet before I needed to stop and rest. I decided that would be far enough for the first day because I was by myself, and I was a little frightened of how fatigued I was after such a short distance. I promised myself I would go back the next day and try again. For the next couple of weeks, I slowly worked my way around the lake. I would stop at each of the benches and rest before I headed to the next bench.

The first time I made it completely around the lake, I wanted to jump for joy. It was such a huge accomplishment for me. I knew I would be able to go back to work without the oxygen tank. I was motivated to keep walking because I knew I needed something to counter-attack the stress and strife to which I would be returning.

I was still under the impression that no one at work knew I had never made it to Arizona to buy that house. Initially I'd planned to go back to work as originally scheduled and never let on that anything was wrong. Luckily for me, I had a cardiac team who convinced me that I had not rebuilt my stamina enough, and I still needed more time to heal.

I was not at all happy when I had to call my boss and tell him what was going on. It felt like I was confessing some huge character defect, and I was still upset and agitated over what happened with doing so poorly on the inspection just before I got sick. It took me two days to build up the courage I actually needed to make the call.

The same day I called him, my boss dropped off the FMLA paperwork. He sat at my dining room table and told me he would support me in whatever way he could. He assured me everything would be taken care of at work until I could get back on my feet. He was surprised when

I told him my doctors felt I needed a few more weeks to recover. They had suggested I start back to work part-time the second week in November. He told me he had to verify that I had enough sick leave available to cover the time frame, and he would get back to me.

He called me the next day and told me he submitted the paperwork, and the sheriff approved my leave. Later the same day, the sheriff called me himself. He told me he was disappointed because I had not let anyone from the agency know I had been so sick. He said that if he had known, he and his wife would have been there to support me. I thanked him for his concern. I started to tell him how bad I felt about how the inspection turned out, and he cut me off. He said something to the effect of, "Don't worry about it. I'm not concerned about it at all. We'll just learn from it."

The sheriff urged me to do whatever was necessary to take care of myself, and that he and his wife would both be available if I needed anything. When I hung up, I felt an old twinge of loyalty and hope that even though the inspection had not gone well, maybe our professional relationship was going to be okay.

CHAPTER 23

— ✐ —

I was grateful that I'd still had almost a full bank of sick leave when my vacation began. I had plenty of leave available on top of the vacation/comp time I'd already used. Knowing that helped me cement my decision that it was time to learn how to take care of myself and put my needs first. It took me another five weeks to begin to feel I was strong enough both physically and emotionally to go back to work.

In the second week of November, I started back to work part-time. My doctor's release was to work up to four hours a day for the first week and slowly increase my time over the next two weeks.

I had quite a few people stop by my office in that first week back. They told me they were glad to see me and happy that I was back. A few of them even scolded me because I didn't let them know how sick I was. Even stranger, a few of them said no one would tell them why I was absent. I had three or four people tell me they'd heard when the inspection hadn't gone well, that I was immediately fired. A few of them asked directly about what the sheriff or my boss said to me at the end of the audit. I assured them I was told we were just going to learn from our mistakes as an agency and move on.

It took me about three weeks to get back into working a full ten-hour day, and on most days, by the time I was done working, I was too tired to do much of anything else.

I began to feel comfortable with being back at work. There were policies that needed revision, and I spent most of my time working to make sure the policy changes were ready for command staff review. I also had a couple of staff inspections due to be completed before the end of the calendar year and spent quite a bit of time preparing for them.

I could sense there was something going on; there were a lot more closed-door meetings. I couldn't quite put my finger on what was happening, and when I questioned my co-workers, they said something was in the works, but no one had told them the details. I knew the guy in the office next door to me knew what was going on, because he acted strangely and avoided eye contact, but I had no idea what was about to happen.

At the end of December, I got a phone call from my boss asking me to meet him in the undersheriff's office in an hour. I asked him what was going on, and he said we'd talk about it shortly. I had a sick feeling in the pit of my stomach. My intuition told me that whatever was happening was not going to be in my best interest. That next hour was one of the longest of my life.

I hated not having any idea what I was facing. In the past, I would have gone to my boss's office to be briefed about what he thought was going on so we could go into the undersheriff's office on the same page. This time, he had not asked me to see him first, and made it seem he was not interested in talking with me before the meeting.

Finally, I went upstairs and walked up to the undersheriff's secretary and told her I was supposed to meet with him. The door to his office was closed, but she told me to knock and go in, so I did.

When I walked in, he asked me to shut the door behind me and have a seat. He started the conversation by telling me over the last few months the command staff had been talking about how to handle the "problem with accreditation." He proceeded to tell me that my boss—the same man who had sat at my dining room table and assured me he would take care of me—had written a proposal while I was gone that would change the structure of the Accreditation Section.

The undersheriff explained that the sheriff and command staff had already approved the proposal, and although the Section had been my responsibility for many years, I was not going to have any say in the new structure.

He told me that sometime after the first of the year, they were going to have one person manage all five of the accreditation processes. Instead of me, that person was going to be a new deputy inspector assigned to the Professional Standards Unit. Since technically I hadn't done anything wrong, they were not actually demoting me and my pay would remain the same. They were, however, reassigning my position to an administrative clerk position, which was more than two pay grades below my current level. They would continue to pay me top management wages, but

I would have clerical responsibilities. Additionally, they would move two other clerks over to work with me.

He went on to explain that the person selected to be the new deputy inspector/accreditation manager was the sergeant currently working in the office next to me. The two clerks I would be working with were the two clerks who currently worked on the jail and medical section accreditation processes, respectively. He also told me they would be remodeling the offices in our area of the building and turning the current Law Enforcement Library into the Accreditation Offices with the three of us clerks sharing an office.

It would take a couple of months for the construction to be complete, so in the meantime, they would move me into a cubicle outside of my old office.

I was stunned and numb. When he asked me if I had any questions, my only reply was, "Why?" He explained that the sheriff was upset about not getting a perfect score on the inspection.

He asked me if I had any other questions. I shook my head and replied, "You know, that I know, there is nothing I can do about this. If it's what the sheriff wants, then I have no choice but to do it." At that time I was still a few years away from collecting retirement, and it would have been financially stupid for me to quit my job. I asked him if there was anything else, and he said, "No."

I got up and walked out the door with my head held high. I did not shut the door, but before I left the area I heard the door slam behind me.

I wondered if they'd thought I would have a complete

and total meltdown, or even collapse. There was no way in hell I would give them the satisfaction of knowing how upset I was. There were a few people standing in the area, so I put on my invisibility mask and walked out the door. Thankfully, there was a private bathroom right outside the admin area, and I was able to get there and shut the door before I broke down and cried my eyes out.

I wasn't sure what to do next, but I decided the smartest thing for me to do was to leave the building. I grabbed my purse and headed out the back door. I wasn't sure where to go, but I knew I needed to get the hell out of there before I did or said something I would regret. I didn't ask anyone's permission to leave, and for the first time in my career, I walked out of that door feeling like a complete and total failure.

I did everything I knew to do to keep my emotions in check as I walked to my car. I needed to create some distance in order to regroup. I felt completely alone and was not sure where to turn. There was no one at the office I could reach out to for support. I decided the best thing to do would be to call my therapist and see if she could fit me in for an emergency session. Thankfully, she did.

By the time I finished telling Jude what happened, I was exhausted, and I knew I would not be able to walk back in the office again that day. She told me to take the next couple of days off and let myself have time to process what had happened. It helped when she told me if I needed a doctor to fill out another FMLA form, she would be more than happy to fill out anything I needed. I called my boss's office and left him a voicemail stating I would be out of the office "sick" until Monday.

I spent the next few days vacillating between rage and utter despair. I knew there was nothing I could do. I was over three years away from being able to collect early retirement. The more I processed what happened, the more I began to see how letting go of all the responsibility could be a blessing in disguise. With the change, I would be able to focus all of my energy on rebuilding my health.

I began to see a way to turn this change to my benefit. If they were willing to pay me management wages to be a clerk, who was I to stop them? I could spend the next three years copying reports, highlighting them, and laughing my way to the bank. I was still upset, but I saw a potential light at the end of the tunnel.

CHAPTER 24

— *♪♪* —

At the beginning of January in 2010, Michael called me and asked me to go to lunch. I thought about it for a minute and decided that with everything that had happened in my life, I was at a point where I could accept him for who and what he was. Over the last couple of years our relationship had completely shifted. I had let go of my dream of ever having anything more with him. He no longer held the same place in my heart, but I still cared about him as a person. I agreed to have lunch for those reasons—and out of curiosity—because he said he needed my help with something.

I could tell right away as we sat and talked that he hadn't changed because his stories were the same. Everything he said still felt inflated. I felt sorry for him as I realized how sad his life actually was. I told him about what had happened at work, and he was outraged and jokingly offered to "sic the Indians" on the sheriff. I told him it was tempting, and we laughed. We immediately switched back to what was going on with him. He half-jokingly said, "Even though I'm a complete asshole, I hope you will still do a favor for my brother."

Curious as to what was going on, I said, "Probably."

It turned out Lance was applying to become the Executive Director of the State of Colorado Indian Affairs Agency. The more Michael told me about the position, the more I knew it would be a perfect fit for Lance. He went on to flatter me and told me if there was anyone who could help Lance navigate the government bureaucracy, it would be me.

I've always had a soft spot in my heart for Lance, so it was a no-brainer for me to agree to help him. It felt good to be needed by someone.

Even though the romantic pull had disappeared with Michael, I was still curious about his family. I had spent too many years hearing all about them but never got to know them, and this was finally my chance to get to know Lance.

Within a couple of days, Lance and I connected via email because he was down in Oklahoma. Lance had been sick for a couple weeks and had gone down to a Native American hospital for medical treatment. While Lance was away, I began to work on his résumé.

I looked forward to getting to know Lance better. In addition to working directly with him, I finally had access to a few of Michael's other friends to ask them to write letters of recommendation for him. In the emails, I suggested possible ways for them to say the things that would make a good impression. We were all invested in Lance getting that position. As a result of working on this project together, I began to notice I no longer had the need for Michael's friends' approval.

Suddenly, Michael and I were back to daily communications, although there was no longer a feeling of intimacy. As the application process continued, Lance's illness worsened. Luckily his parents lived near a hospital in Oklahoma where he could get the medical care he needed. He, his wife, and son could stay with his parents while he recuperated. Lance sent me an email and told me he would get back to me with the changes for his application when he felt better.

In the meantime, Michael kept me informed about what went on with Lance. As it turned out, what he thought was pneumonia was the precursor to a heart attack. Once the doctors determined it was a heart issue, they ran tests and decided Lance needed bypass surgery. Because they'd waited so long to diagnose his condition, he was already very weak, and the surgery was going to be high risk.

I had just stopped by Michael's job to give him some paperwork for Lance when he got the phone call that Lance was not going to make it. In a series of unfortunate illness-related events, he ultimately died. We were both in shock.

I've always believed the universe put us together that night to make sure Michael had someone to lean on while he dealt with both the emotional and pragmatic issues around Lance's death.

CHAPTER 25

— ♪♪ —

The next morning I experienced an event I hesitate to share. I was sitting in a church for a 12-Step meeting the morning after Lance died, saying the opening prayer with my eyes closed. I sensed something in front of me and opened my eyes, there appeared to be a puff of smoke right in front of my face.

It surprised me that someone was smoking in a church, yet there was no odor. I looked around to see if anyone else had sensed it, and no one else seemed to notice. I knew the smoke was a message from Lance. Deep inside my soul I heard the message, "Tell Michael I am okay, that everything will be okay, and don't worry or be too upset."

I was in shock. It took me a couple of minutes to let it sink in. Was I willing to believe Lance actually came to me? Was it some kind of optical illusion? Although I eventually stopped doubting what happened, I continued to doubt Michael would believe or accept the message, especially from a white woman. But, no matter what he believed, I had to at least try to convey Lance's message to him.

I thought about it and decided to take Michael out to

the Tall Bull Memorial Park where there's a herd of buffalo kept near sacred Native American grounds. Whether he believed me or not about Lance's message, it would give Michael a chance to pray with the animals he considered his brothers.

When we got to the buffalo herd, I told Michael I would wait for him in the car as he took care of whatever he needed to do. I sat and prayed, asking for guidance on how to bring the subject up to Michael in a way he might be able to hear it. As soon as he was done praying and got back into my car, I told him I doubted he would believe me, but I was going to tell him something. With tears in my eyes, I passed on Lance's message. Shockingly, he looked at me and said he did believe Lance contacted him through me. It gave me a deep sense of relief to have Michael believe me.

On our way back to Michael's house from Tall Bull, Michael asked me to go to Lance's memorial at the Denver Indian Center. I told him I would be honored to go and asked him if I could bring a friend with me because I didn't want to sit alone and knew he would be busy with his official duties. The friend I chose to go with me was a woman that I had only known for a few months, but she knew Michael and I had a history. She was a good enough friend to agree to go without asking a lot of questions. She told me later how honored she was to be there with me.

It was the first time I was welcomed to sit inside a sacred circle at the Indian Center. Although the ceremony was very sad and very intense, it felt good to be included on the inside. Ironically, I no longer had the same strong need to be included in the community, and yet, there I was.

I was astonished when Michael openly acknowledged me during his eulogy for Lance. He explained to his community that I was helping Lance apply for the job at Colorado Indian Affairs, and he would be forever grateful to me for all I had done. By the time Michael was done talking about what Lance had meant to him and the Denver Native American community, there was not a dry eye in the house. Michael's talk was followed by many others expressing how saddened they were by Lance's sudden departure from this physical world. There were a few laughs mixed in because Lance would have wanted them to remember his light-hearted side, too. The ceremony was one of the most moving events I have ever witnessed.

After the memorial service, there was a full Native American feast, and although we were invited, my friend and I chose to leave. We stopped to say good-bye to Michael and tell him we thought he'd done a wonderful job paying tribute to his brother. I was speechless when he stepped forward and gave me a huge hug in the middle of the Indian Center. He merely said, "Thanks," but the gesture was a huge step toward healing our past.

CHAPTER 26

— ♒ —

On the following Monday morning, I was driving to work thinking about Michael on his way to Oklahoma to bury Lance's body. As I drove down a highway off-ramp to go to my office, a similar "puff of smoke" appeared on the passenger side of my car. It was at that moment I *KNEW* deep in my soul that life was too short to be miserable and it was time for me to walk away from the insanity and stress at work.

It felt like Lance came to me twice, once to pass a message on to Michael, and once with a message specifically for me. I have always believed that Lance could see beyond the color of my skin and the size of my body and saw directly into my soul. Having him visit from beyond confirmed that feeling for me. I knew he was there supporting me from the other side in the same way I had offered to support him in trying to find a job. His presence reminded me that life was way too precious to continue to live in a way that no longer served anyone. It was time to break myself out of my self-imposed prison.

When I got to the office that morning and settled down in my cubicle, I knew there was no way I could ignore the spiritual message from Lance. I didn't tell anyone at work what happened with the smoke, or that I was considering leaving my job.

It was the experience in my car that gave me the confidence to make the phone call to my financial advisor to determine what I needed to do to take early retirement. Up until that moment, I had planned to continue to collect almost $90,000 a year to do a clerk's job. I wasn't exactly sure how I was going survive financially. But at that moment I knew there was no way in hell I could continue walking through the doors of what felt like a prison to me. I knew I had to find my own "get out of jail free" card and play it.

I'd inherited some assets from my parents, and I was possibly in a position to support myself until I could build my own business. I wouldn't know for sure, though, until I sat down with my financial advisor to talk through my options.

I'd spent the last couple of months playing the role of good girl while the administration continued to put the new Accreditation structure in place, and technically I was still the Accreditation Manager. It took longer than any of them wanted it to because I needed to train my replacement, and he had to train his replacement, plus they were in the middle of construction for the new office space.

No one was surprised when I magnanimously offered to run to get coffee for my co-workers, but my primary motivation was to make a phone call. On my way to the coffee shop, I made an appointment to explore my retirement options. My financial advisor had an appointment available in a couple of days. She told me what documents to gather to bring along, and I finally felt like I had the beginnings of a new lease on life.

When we sat down the following Friday to look at my options, I decided to rearrange some investments, and reallocate the money I was going to use to buy investment property in Sedona. It would take several days for all the paperwork to go through. In the meantime she helped me see that I could successfully build-up a business and bridge the financial gap between April of 2010 and May of 2013 when my pension kicked in.

As soon as I was done gathering the pragmatic data, I set up an appointment with my psychologist. Talking to Jude seemed like a good move while I navigated my plan. After we had chatted, I decided I would not tell anyone what I planned until all the finances were in place. She helped me to realize that after all my years of attempting to meet my dad's expectations, my inheritance from my parents now supported me in my dreams of becoming more authentically myself.

For the next couple of weeks, it became fun to play the political game at work because I knew the end was in sight. I did not tell a single soul beyond my financial advisor and my therapist what I planned to do. As far as everyone else knew, I was just happily rolling with the punches.

It took ten days for all the financial maneuvering to fall into place. With secret delight, I spent about a week at home composing my letter of resignation. They still had not made the official change of positions at work, technically I held the title of the Accreditation Manager, and I could use it on my letter of resignation. It soothed my ego to retire with my title intact.

Technically, I should have submitted the letter up the chain-of-command to either my direct supervisor or to Human Resources. But I had no desire to talk to the man who stabbed me in the back. I wasn't going to give him or the undersheriff the satisfaction of being able to take the news to the sheriff.

Once the funds were completely liquid, and my future was secure, I'd take the letter directly to the sheriff myself. Each day, as I waited, I would print a new copy of my letter of resignation with that day's date.

I picked the retirement date of April 8th because it was the last workday prior to my 48th birthday. When I chose that date, I cemented my eligibility to collect my pension in May of 2013. That would give them three weeks to figure out what they wanted to do to fill the soon-to-be-created new clerical position.

Finally, the day had come. The funds were in the bank and I walked upstairs to ask the sheriff's secretary to make an appointment to see him. I was surprised when she said, "He's in his office now if you want to knock and see if he'll see you."

He looked surprised to see me, but agreed to let me come in. I asked to close his door and proceeded to hand him my letter. I had clearly caught him off guard. He paused for a few seconds as he digested what he was reading. I felt a little gratification knowing that I had blindsided him. Apparently, he'd bought into my acting normal during the last few weeks. All of those years of watching how the political game was played had paid off, and, for a fleeting moment, I had the upper hand. I doubt he thought I would stop playing the game, and had not anticipated I would be willing take a huge leap of faith and fly solo for three years without the illusion of the safety net of a paycheck.

His first comment was something to the effect of, "I sure hope you know what you're doing, because this is a stupid decision." I kept my composure for the first few minutes of the conversation. I explained to him what had happened with my health back in September, combined with the recent unexpected death of someone close to me, had helped me to see that life is too short. I clarified it had been a difficult decision, but it was time to begin to live my life and to build my own dreams.

I told him the final straw was when both my boss and the undersheriff told me he was deeply disappointed in me. I cried as I told him I was sorry I had let him down, and I had been just as disappointed by the results of the inspection as he had. He tried to tell me when he made the decision to reorganize accreditation it had nothing to do with my performance. Hence, they had not changed my pay.

I told him they would not be happy I'd bypassed the chain-of-command and didn't let them know what I was doing before I talked with him. Part of me hoped he would ask what it would take for me to stay. I was fully prepared to tell him there was nothing he could do because I had put a lot of thought into my decision. Yet, there was a small part of me that would have liked for him to at least ask, but he didn't.

We talked for about thirty minutes. At the end of the conversation, he told me he understood why I was making the move, and he even offered to write me a letter of recommendation. As I walked out of his office he told me he wished me well. Although I knew deep down he was a consummate politician, I left his office believing what he said.

Sadly, five years later, I have not had another conversation with him, the undersheriff, or my captain. I was completely ignored by all three of them as I ended my twenty-six-year career.

The next three weeks went by in a blur as I attempted to teach my replacement what he needed to know. In the end, on the final day of my employment, the lieutenant assigned to Internal Affairs presented me with my retirement plaque. There was a small gathering in our new accreditation office where some of my work friends gave me parting gifts, but no one from command staff came by to say goodbye. It felt like another insult from them.

A couple of weeks later, the Rocky Mountain Accreditation Network had a retirement luncheon for me. I was honored and deeply moved when a sheriff from a different agency, a couple of police chiefs, and numerous police commanders in attendance all said kind things about me, but it was bittersweet because the only representatives from my own agency were a sergeant and the two new accreditation clerks.

A couple of my colleagues told me my agency's command staff's lack of attendance reflected more poorly on the administration than it did on me. It was nice to hear, but it was still hurtful to me. In the end, it merely cemented my decision that it was time for me to move on.

They say the best revenge is to live a good life, and after I'd left the agency, freedom began to set in, and my life began to change dramatically.

CHAPTER 27

— ♫ —

Initially, I found myself alternating between exhaustion and exhilaration over the weeks following my resignation. On my last day at work, as I left the secure parking area for the last time, I pulled out a thermos of margaritas. Sipping the salty-sweet concoction, I toasted the assholes as I left. It was my one last odd attempt of rebellion and felt like my own personal little "screw you" to the rules of the agency.

After I gave up the big paycheck from my job, my therapist and I both knew I would not be able to continue to pay hundreds of dollars a month for therapy. She helped me to create an exit strategy over the next few weeks. She suggested I attend more 12-Step meetings, partly because they are free, and more importantly, she knew I needed the connection with people. It was time for me to stop isolating and begin finding a group of like-minded people. Going to 12-Step meetings seemed like a relatively simple solution.

Part of me dreaded ending therapy. Jude had been a lifeline for me during some of the darkest times in my life. I knew I would always be grateful to her for her compassion and her wisdom. We spent the last few sessions talking about how my decision-making process had improved. She told me she was no longer concerned about the choices I was making on a day-to-day basis. She could see that I had started putting my needs first.

During my last appointment, Jude told me how proud she was of me and acknowledged all of the changes I had made in my life. For the first time, she voiced the concerns she'd previously held for Michael and me. She told me that before I ended my relationship with him she'd been concerned I was going to let him move into my house and live off of me both financially and emotionally. We both laughed as she told me how relieved she was when I finally woke up to the dysfunction of that relationship.

In many ways, during my last therapy session, I felt like I was graduating. She let me know she'd always be available to me if I ran into trouble, but she was confident I was ready to face the world without her. I walked out of her office deeply and profoundly grateful and proud, knowing she wasn't concerned about the choices I'd be making in the world. I felt like a five-year-old skipping on the playground, finally ready to take responsibility for making healthier decisions for my life.

The next few months went by in a haze. I hadn't wanted to acknowledge I was still energetically depleted and had no idea how long it was going to take to get completely restored. Initially, I had set aside six weeks to regain my all of my energy. I hadn't realized it was going to be a much slower process.

I was still learning how to put my needs first. My circadian clock still had me waking up every morning at

4:45 a.m. It took a few weeks of waking up and starting to get out of bed until it dawned on me that I didn't have to get up and go to the Sheriff's Office ever again. Each time the realization hit I was both relieved and saddened. I had never dreamt my career would end on such a miserable note.

After a while, I slowly developed a new daily routine. For those first weeks, I wandered around my life in a state of emotional confusion. I was relieved to be away from the stress and anxiety of my job, but I also missed the structure that came from government work. It hadn't been the healthiest environment, but it was one in which, after twenty-six years, I knew how to navigate. All of a sudden, everything in my life felt upside down and backwards.

I found a 12-Step clubhouse a couple of miles from my house with multiple meetings every day. My favorite meeting started at 6:45 a.m., so I decided to start my day with that meeting. It didn't take long before I found both a new way of life and a new circle of friends. I am not going to share a lot of details to stay within the tradition of the program's anonymity, but I will say the people I met from that particular clubhouse were the first people who accepted me completely and fully for who I was. Although my issues with alcohol were not as intense as my issues with food/sugar, they accepted me in to their fold. Ironically it was not in spite of my flaws, but because of them.

I had a lot of time on my hands to attend meetings during those first few months of being away from my job, and attended multiple meetings a day. Before I knew it, I was starting to come back to life. I will always be grateful to the people in those meetings who were the foundation of my physical, emotional, and spiritual recovery.

Over the next couple of years Michael and I continued to talk occasionally. Our conversations were usually the same old stuff; he would tell me about his life and try to make me laugh. I would share some of the new events in my life, but in reality we no longer had much in common, and once again we slowly drifted apart.

CHAPTER 28

— *ॐ* —

During this time, I started working with a hypnotherapist to help me release some of the old subconscious emotional patterns from my past.

After I had done some healing with hypnotherapy, I decided to pursue training as a hypnotherapist. My hypnotherapist introduced me to her teacher, and I began training in Cellular Release Therapy™. At the same time, I enrolled in basic hypnotherapy training and attended the Colorado Coaching and Hypnotherapy Training Institute (CCHTI), where I became certified as both a Hypnotherapist and as a Hypnotic Coach.

During my CCHTI training, I was introduced to a modality known as Radiant Heart Therapy. It was created by a woman who has documented the significant impact of heart-centered healing in the world and created a unique process that enhances hypnosis.

Initially, I planned to become a hypnotherapist specializing in Cellular Release Therapy. I completed all of my certifications and fulfilled the requirements to be a Registered Psychotherapist in the State of Colorado.

As I began to shift the focus of my business, I renamed

my company Find Serenity & Empowerment specializing in Hypnotic Coaching. My Hypnosis mentor and I had realized that although the hypnotherapy model was powerful, the Hypnotic-Coaching model was a much better match for my personality. Hypnotic-coaching is a solution-focused coaching technique better suited for less serious psycho-emotional problems and life stressors. The coach and the client co-create a life change that is purposeful, focused and successful.

CHAPTER 29

— ✍ —

After a while, I realized one of the few things I missed from my old career was writing. It was the only creative outlet I'd had at the Sheriff's Office. It had taken me some time to recognize how much I enjoyed finding the right words to use in law enforcement policy, and that writing policy had actually been a creative writing endeavor.

As I acknowledged missing writing, I began linking it to the resentments I still held about the way my career ended. I started to formulate the fantasy of writing a tell-all exposé on all of the horrific things I had seen and experienced at the Sheriff's Office. I started down a path of, "I'll make them suffer. I'll tell the world about what was going on behind the scenes."

The timing seemed perfect; the Pat Sullivan scandal had just hit the news. The first sheriff I had worked for was arrested for trading meth for sex with young men, and housed in the jail that had been named after him in 2002. The local news was having a field day talking about the how the former super-hero had turned villain, and I had had a front row seat for many years. Part of me wanted to "set the record straight," but thankfully fate intervened and I didn't have to.

One such fateful Sunday morning, I was watching Oprah's Super Soul Sunday, and they were showing the film *Fierce Grace*, which was about Ram Dass's life in his later years. In the movie, there's a scene in which Ram Dass hired a writing editor to help him finish a book manuscript that was delayed because of his stroke.

As I watched the movie, I was enthralled with the energy of the particular man they hired to work with Ram Dass to finish his book. I witnessed a deep compassion in this man. I was impressed with the balance he had between being respectful of Ram Dass for the celebrity he was, and the need to coach him to do the story telling. They showed his name (Mark Matousek) on the screen, and I followed my instinct and looked him up online. On his website, I noticed he offered different types of assistance to writers including writing classes.

I composed a short email and asked him for information on his upcoming classes. I told him I was seriously thinking about writing a book, and I would like to talk with him about what resources I would need. The next day, he answered my email and suggested we talk on the phone; we arranged our first phone meeting later that week.

When we spoke, I told him about my deep desire to write a tell-all expose of the dirty politics at the Sheriff's Office. I verbally shared the outline of my story. He described several different options that would help me move forward. The option that made the most sense to both of us was to join one of his online writing classes.

The class had been created to help people craft their stories and get used to writing. Once a week, for ten weeks, Mark gave the group a subject/topic to discuss, usually spiritually related, and each member of the group was to write a thousand-word essay. The writing could be submitted to the entire group or privately to him.

Initially, I was a little leery about writing in front of a group of strangers about deeply sensitive subjects. Mark assured me that if I were going to write a book, I would need to get used to having other people read my work.

He created the class with the expectation that it was to be a safe, respectful environment. For those of us who chose to submit to the group of fifteen people, he set guidelines for commenting on each other's writing, discouraging us from critiquing each other's work.

Our first assignment was to discuss the deepest secret you tell yourself. He explained that most of us lie to ourselves more than we lie to others. I was surprised to see he jumped right into the deep-end of my life in the very first assignment during the very first week. I was tempted to change my mind and not write, but I talked myself into writing the thousand words. I was tempted to submit the work to him privately because I didn't want to reveal my biggest lie to a group of total strangers, but I talked myself into submitting it the entire group.

The feedback I received from him, and the support I got from the others in the group, was astounding. There was a certain level of anonymity in writing in an online class that created an environment where it felt safe to disclose intimate details about my life.

Those of us who chose to share our writing became very close and supportive of each other. During the class we found out we were all from different locations, and none of us knew each other before we started the class. By the end, there was a group of ten of us who decided to continue our new friendship outside of class and we subsequently created a private Facebook group to do just that.

Between Mark's guidance during the writing classes and the interaction with my new group of writing buddies, I realized I didn't need to write the tell-all exposé of the dirty secrets of my previous employer. By then I had developed enough spiritual faith to know that karma and divine law would take care of the situation for me. I slowly began to learn how to stop living in the past.

Through my writing, I saw how the resentment I carried was no longer serving me. I began to see my role in all of my experiences and slowly began to forgive others and myself for the circumstances of my past. It took some time for me to see the events at the end of my career were just one part of the tapestry of my life. I was gradually starting to understand that without all of the experiences of my life, I would not be the person I'd become.

It was a tremendous time of growth and change in my life, and I will always be grateful to Mark and my fellow writers.

The ten of us from my first class have continued to use a private Facebook group to remain in close contact. They are truly part of my soul family. Over the years, many of us have traveled to meet face-to-face. We've stayed at each other's homes and held each other's hearts during times of great sorrow and times of great joy. A couple of years ago, one of them coined the phrase "SoulTen." We have a dream of having all ten of us in one location at the same time, and I hold the space in my future for that to happen. I am beyond grateful to my SoulTen for everything.

CHAPTER 30

—— ✿ ——

In July of 2012, as I built my new life, I received an opportunity to go to Las Vegas to present my first professionally-promoted workshop. I was invited to present a workshop on *Health at Every Size* for plus-size women as a part of a convention.

There were over three hundred people registered for the event. It felt like a great way to step up in the world and promote the newest side of my business and, frankly, of myself. I experienced a great deal of self-doubt as the workshop approached. Although there were a lot of people registered for the overall event, I had no idea how many people would attend my workshop. The organizer told me because it was Las Vegas, and there are so many other activities like gambling available, attendance could be as few as ten and as many as the full three hundred.

As I prepared my presentation, I realized it didn't matter how many people were in the room. I knew it was my opportunity to step out in the world as my new authentic, heart-centered, healing self. I had begun to loosen my invisibility cloak.

Presenting to large groups of people was not new to

me. I had been facilitating accreditation-related workshops for large groups of cops for many years. But in order for me to stand up in front of those cops, I always felt like I was pretending to be an expert in my field. Although I had the credentials to present and teach the materials I discussed, I had never felt truly authentic.

As a part of my healing journey, I promised myself I would make it a priority to be as authentic as I could be. The days of wearing a mask to get someone else's approval or to meet a perceived expectation needed to be behind me. The opportunity to present the workshop felt like the universe had conspired to show me how far I'd progressed.

I was nervous getting ready for the event, but once my presentation started and I connected with the group, my nerves settled down. It turned out to be a small group of people, and the organizer apologized for the turnout, but I assured her it all worked out exactly the way it was supposed to.

After my presentation, a couple of people approached me to hire me as their coach. More importantly, I felt as if I were finally stepping into the world as the authentic person I was meant to be.

CHAPTER 31

— ♪♫ —

I had been home from Las Vegas a couple of weeks when my life took yet another unexpected turn.

The morning of July 26, 2012, I picked up my phone and found a voice message from a woman who said she was a friend of Michael's. She had been asked to pass on information that Michael may not live through the day. I was aware Michael's health had not been good the last few months, but I was under the impression he was at home healing from a lung infection that had him hospitalized when I last saw him in April. It seemed impossible that our friendship had gotten that far away from me.

As I sat and wondered what had happened, I reluctantly decided the next right move would be to call the woman back. I listened and grasped that Michael was in a hospital within a couple of miles of me. I decided just to start driving over to the hospital as I listened to her.

I had a fleeting thought about my appearance, because I was still terribly sweaty from having just finished my workout. I wasn't wearing any makeup, my oily hair was up in a ponytail, and I was still in my workout clothes. I desperately needed a shower. Normally, I wouldn't have been caught dead in public looking that way, yet my intuition said I needed to go to the hospital right away.

I formulated a plan to make a quick stop at the hospital and run up to ICU to check on Michael's condition. My idea was to go upstairs and talk with a nurse to find out what was going on and then go home, take a shower, and come back later in the day to visit him.

He was in the hospital where I had visited many other friends, so the layout was familiar to me. I knew exactly how to walk into ICU undetected. All it took was an attitude of confidence and acting as if I knew exactly where I was going. My plan was working well until I realized I didn't know which of the cubicle rooms Michael was in.

I asked at the nurse's station instead of peering into each room. A pleasant, compassionate-looking nurse turned around and said, "May I help you?" I told her who I was looking for, and her expression changed drastically. Her face became strained, and I think she even looked a little pale. She didn't utter a word, and merely pointed behind her to the corner room.

As soon as I turned around, I knew exactly why she had had such a strange reaction. I could see inside the small glassed-in ICU cubicle. Michael was easy to spot, but what stopped me in my tracks were the eight Native Americans standing around his crowded room quietly singing and drumming. I was nervous because I couldn't tell for sure whether or not Michael was still alive. Walking in that room as the sole white woman would be walking into territory previously forbidden.

As I stood waiting for my feet to move me forward, I recognized a few of the faces of the people singing to him, and once again, none of them knew me. I knew most of them by name and their relationships to Michael. I recognized everyone except the heavily-tattooed Indian woman sitting beside his bed crying. I stopped momentarily with my feet frozen to the floor, not exactly sure how to proceed.

As I stood there, I was actually more surprised by who was NOT in the room. Michael's drum/singing group friends were not at his side. Other than his sister and his nephew, the people I had known to be his family and his closest friends were not with him. I simply could not imagine why they were absent.

For a few long seconds, I had an internal battle as to whether or not I was going to open the glass door and walk in. There was a strong possibility I would not be allowed by the Indians to enter. I feared once again that the color of my skin could interfere with my relationship with Michael. Taking a deep breath of courage, I opened the door.

As I walked into his ICU cubicle, at first I couldn't tell for sure whether Michael was conscious, or even still alive. He was lying very still with his eyes closed as the group of Indians sang a ceremonial song. There were tubes in his nose and mouth. The woman sitting at the far side of his bed continued to cry. As I walked in, the elder in charge of the ceremony said, "May we help you?" with an authoritative "What the hell are you doing in here?" kind of tone.

I looked at him and said, "I'm Sue Relihan, Michael's friend from Arapahoe Sheriff."

As I said the words, Michael's eyes opened, and he reached his hand out to me. I stepped up to the bed and took his hand. The woman on the other side of the bed saw Michael recognize me, and simply said, "Thank you for coming, he can't talk because of the tubes." She put her head down and started crying again.

I held Michael's hand as I told him I was sorry I hadn't known he was so ill. I explained I had been out of town and had just heard what was happening. I apologized for showing up unkempt, and that I had rushed right over when I heard what was going on.

I made a bold move and put my hand on his stomach, and I told him how grateful I was to have been in his life. The woman on the other side of the bed looked up and gave me a slightly suspicious look as it became obvious Michael and I had a deep connection.

Although his breathing tube kept him from speaking, his eyes and his unwillingness to let go of my hand told me he was very glad to see me. He looked at me with love, and I knew he was very grateful I had come to say good-bye.

Over the next forty-minutes, I stood by his bedside while they sang to him. Before I realized what was happening they stopped singing, and his new companion asked him if he was ready. It took a minute for me to comprehend part of the ceremony was over, and she asked him if he was ready for them to turn off the respirator. He nodded.

The hospital staff came in and took him off the

respirator. It never once crossed my mind to leave his side, and I stood at the foot of his bed with the others. With a small group of his Indian friends singing him across and his sister holding on to his nephew who cradled his head, Michael took his last breath.

The elder told us it was time to complete the ceremony and smudge Michael's body. I was surprised the hospital was going to allow them to smudge him. They explained to me that they had made arrangements with the chaplain the night before to be able to do the ceremony, and the hospital had agreed. However, the nurse panicked when she realized they were about to light a match near all of the oxygen in Cardiac ICU and immediately alerted the hospital administrator, the hospital chaplain, and security.

Apparently the hospital administrator who agreed to the ceremony had not realized that the ceremony included smudging, which consisted of lighting a stick of sweet grass and sage with a match.

The chaplain followed closely by a security guard came in to the room and tried to explain the hospital had changed its mind and forbade the lighting of the smudge stick in ICU.

Michael's friends and family looked like they were about to do it regardless of the hospital rules. I knew at that moment one of the reasons I had somehow been guided to the hospital was to be a bridge between the Indians and the hospital administration. I knew the hospital could not put the other patients and staff at risk, but the Indians were hell-bent on performing the ceremony, especially since they'd already received permission.

I spent the next several minutes helping negotiate between the two sides until we reached an agreement. As a compromise, the Indians were allowed to move Michael's body, in his hospital bed, without covering his face, through different floors of the hospital and outside to a back dock area. It took two different elevators going to different levels before he reached his destination.

Once Michael's body was outside in a relatively secluded space, it was time for Michael's nephew to perform the smudging ceremony. I'd walked outside with the family to make sure everything worked out okay. I had planned to step away while they performed the smudging, but as his nephew prayed and smudged Michael's body, he began to smudge the family members and, much to my surprise, he included me. Until that point, I had managed to stay strong and stoic as the events unfolded. After being smudged I stood by his body with mixed feelings and with tears rolling down my face.

Slowly I realized that what had been impossible for Michael to give me while he was alive (to let a white woman into his inner Native American circle) became possible with his death.

Ironically, as touched as I was to be a part of the ceremony, it didn't hold nearly the impact on me it would have years ago.

After the smudging ceremony, they wheeled Michael's body back upstairs to the ICU unit. The hospital said it would be okay for his body to lie in wait for a few hours while other members of his family and friends came by to pay their last respects.

Once the ceremony was over, and I felt like I was no longer needed, I was ready to leave. Plus I was about to be overwhelmed with emotion. There was no way I could stay there and freely express the depth and intensity of my emotion. I wasn't ready to explain the extent of my true feelings in front of the people there, so I left.

As I walked out of the hospital, I noticed his sister was standing outside talking with someone. I debated whether I should ask some questions or simply go home. My overwhelming curiosity won out over my more conservative belief of minding my own damn business. I chose to walk up and ask his sister what she knew about Michael's new companion. I was curious about when and how it came to be that she had the legal authority to make all of Michael's final arrangements, and expressed my surprise that she would be making all of his final arrangements with the help of a few of Michael's friends.

Michael's sister told me she didn't know very many details, but she understood Michael had met the woman online about six months before. From her perspective, the woman had shown up suddenly and pretty much ingratiated herself to Michael as he tried to heal from his lung infection. Evidently a few days earlier, Michael legally signed everything over to her.

I also felt a strong urge to ask her about the whereabouts of the people I assumed Michael would have wanted with him at the end. I could not imagine his best friends wouldn't have moved heaven and earth to be there to say good-bye, but I stopped when I could tell my questions made her uncomfortable. She clearly didn't want to say anything negative about anyone and obviously had no reason to believe she could open up to me. I was surprised she hadn't asked me more about who I was, or why Michael was obviously so comfortable with having me at his deathbed. I decided it was better to stop the conversation, because I realized she had more than enough to deal with.

As I drove out of the hospital parking lot, I needed to talk about what just happened. That need was accompanied by a deep sense of frustration that my current circle of friends didn't have a frame of reference for the magnitude of it all. I didn't have the energy to go back to tell them the entire history between Michael and me. It would take too long for them to understand the depth of how I'd felt being present during his death, especially being included in his smudging ceremony.

I decided to call the one person I knew who might be home and would have a deeper understanding of the significance: my sister. She and I hadn't been very close the last few years, but she was around for the beginning of my relationship with Michael. I needed someone with whom I could just start talking, someone who might understand the enormity of my feelings. I was grateful that she was home and answered the phone.

I launched right into my story of what happened during the last few hours. She was appropriately sympathetic and allowed me to keep talking as I processed my feelings. I will always be grateful she was there at the end of the phone line that day.

In many ways, Michael's death shook me to my core because it felt like my life had completed a cycle. In 2003 when I met him, I could never have predicted the path our lives would take. I would have given almost anything in those days to be acknowledged by him and the Native community with the acceptance I felt after he died. It's ironic how, nine years later, when I stumbled upon his deathbed, the deep need to be a part of his inner circle was no longer there.

Don't get me wrong. I was honored to be with him as he transitioned from this life to the next. I was deeply moved when I was included in all of the ceremonies around his death, including his funeral and burial.

In the very end, although he could no longer speak, his eyes had communicated the love he once felt for me. By the end of that week, our relationship truly felt complete.

...And I was no longer invisible.

ABOUT ME AND MY LIFE TODAY

In the period since Michael's death, I have taken a lot of time and energy to review and take inventory of my life. As a result, my life has taken on new meaning, though the path has changed course a couple of times.

I explored many different directions as I uncovered what felt most appropriate for me. For the most part, the journey has been both fun and challenging. Some days were sunny; some were not. My life is in no way perfect. There are still many bumps on my path. Almost everything I do now centers around self-growth, because I realize how important it is for me to continue moving forward. I am still very much a work in progress, and believe I will continue to be on a healing journey until I draw my last breath.

Some of my earlier stress reactions have shown back up because I didn't have all the changes embedded deeply enough into my everyday life. I believe in focusing on my progress, but some days self-acceptance has still been a challenge. Thankfully I'm learning to accept small, steady steps of forward progress. I find that the more patient I am with myself, the more I remove the 'have-to's and replace them with 'I want to's, the happier I am.

Trying to remain invisible and giving my power away almost killed my soul. Today, my number one priority is to express my feelings and set boundaries so that I may be visible and feel confident in the world, therefore I'm available to be helpful to others.

I follow a similar routine every day. I start with meditation and connect with a Universal source much greater than myself. I use this time to set my intentions for the day. I've also learned to keep healthy food choices in the house and make movement a priority.

I believe that continuing to grow both personally and professionally is essential. I attend workshops and training classes as frequently as possible.

In the last few years I have met some of the most remarkable people in the world. I surround myself with people who are dedicated to assisting themselves and others in personal transformation. My old, outdated, conservative law-enforcement-entrained beliefs have been blown out of the water. The old model of fear and competition has happily been replaced with a new model of camaraderie and collaboration.

One of the most profound principles that has stayed with me is an unwavering belief in abundance, both in material ways and in energy. Somehow, in spite of my parent's financial philosophies from The Great Depression, I have always trusted that there would be more than enough money for me. There have been times on my journey when my pot of abundance appeared to be getting low, and each time something happened that refilled the pot.

I contribute a lot of my ability to live in a world full of

abundance to a deep commitment in sharing what I have. Some of my beliefs around sharing were cemented during the years I spent hanging out with Native Americans. I saw them share in ways I have not experienced in other cultures. It started with a deep sense of gratitude for what little they may have had and a willingness to share it with someone else. I try to carry that belief forward in my life today.

I recognize that everything I've experienced has helped shape me into the woman I am. I believe all of my experiences, all of my relationships, all the professional positions I've held, all my therapy sessions, and all of my challenging life events have given me a solid foundation for my life. They are also my greatest source of wisdom.

Hypnotic Coaching is by far the best tool I have come across. Many people have no idea what a Hypnotic Coach does. I love it when I get the opportunity to share information on my profession. Hypnotic coaching is a combination of life coaching and hypnosis designed to reconnect clients with their personal power. After a few sessions, most clients feel a substantial increase in their self-confidence and can maintain a higher degree of focus and determination to reach their goals. Hypnosis adds a powerful boost to the traditional coaching model.

I love watching my clients achieve a goal by overcoming an old, limiting belief that is no longer serving them. Removing their emotional barriers or their negative mindset makes it easier to become the ideal relationship partner, or achieve a higher level of professional success.

I have written this book with the intent of inspiring

others to see that creating a new life is possible. With the exception of the people who have died or have already been identified in the media, I have changed names to provide a level of anonymity.

Even during our darkest times, there truly is a light on the horizon. The journey of transformation can be a bumpy one. The secret is to surround yourself with amazing people not only dedicated to their own journeys, but willing to assist their fellow travelers.

You too can become empowered to live the life of your dreams!

I have created a variety of programs and products. If you believe I can assist you on your journey, please visit www.SueRelihan.com for more information.

GRATITUDE AND ACKNOWLEDGEMENT

Many people have supported me on my self-growth journey the last few years. I wish I could name everyone, but I'm going to risk unintentionally leaving out someone to name a few specific people who have had tremendous impact on my journey.

To my family of origin—my dad Joe, my mom Winifred, and my sister Ruth—I know each of you loved me, as I will always love you. Over the years I have become more and more grateful for the foundation you gave me.

To the men and women I worked with in law enforcement: thank you for ALL of the experiences, without them I would not be the person I am today. It's important to note that the current administration at the Sheriff's Office is not the same administration I worked with. There was another new Sheriff elected in 2014 and from what I hear, he is doing a good job.

To the Denver Native American Community, you may not have known who I was or why I was attending your events, but I have always been grateful to you for everything I have learned about your culture.

To Dr. Judith Meyer, for being there when I believed I didn't have anywhere else to turn. Your guidance kept me going and truly saved my sanity. Thank you for teaching me the true meaning of persistence.

To the medical and healthcare providers who have supported me in getting healthier, I remain forever grateful to each of you. Specifically Dr. Doug Robertson and Dr. David Flitter; the doctors I credit for saving my life on September 1, 2009.

To Susan Luthye, Patti Kelly, and Angela Dutro for being there when I needed you during the darkest moments of my life.

To Stacey Morris who has had a tremendous impact on my healing in the last couple of years, thank you for everything you have done to assist me on my healing journey. I would not be where I am today without your loving, caring, supportive soul.

To my friends at the Dragon's Den, thank you for giving me a safe place to land when it felt like I had nowhere else to turn. Shelley, Chris, Eric, Hanne, Buddy, David, Olive, Randy, Jose, Peter, Rick, Di, Sue, Samantha, Kevin, Nancy, Priscilla, Steve, Erin, Kat, Matt, Shannon, Troy, Valarie, Nancy, Barnes, Jen, Hunter, and the rest of the crew—I am grateful.

To my special circle (SoulTen) of writing friends who have held my heart as I've taken this journey. You are the foundation for my writing. Starting with Mark Matousek, my first writing coach, and his partner David Moore, thank you for everything. Mark introduced me to my SoulTen. These nine people are all very powerful writers in their right, and have each touched my life in ways for which I will be forever grateful: Stacey Cohen, Florence Lombard, Ferebe Conchar, Brenda Hanson, Lynn Herring, Roger McCormick, Sharyl Volpe, GeJa Seeley, and Susie Sawyer. Thank you for providing a sacredly protected place to discover my own soul.

To Faith Young and my sisterhood at Wealthy Women Empowerig Wealthy Women, thank you for holding my heart. I can't imagine my life without each of you in it.

To the writing specialists who helped me to shape my story/book: Pat Verducci, Kris Jordan, Pat Matson, and Kristin Dodds Rose, I could not have done this without each of you.

To Heather Perry and the team at Balboa Press for holding my hand and leading me through the self-publishing maze.

To Mythica von Griffin, thank you for the transformative bodypainting session shown on the front cover of this book.

To Michelle Asaki, I'm grateful for the incredible photography and for creating a beautifully safe environment for me while photographing the sessions.

To Peggy Sands for all of your graphic artist talents. Especially the beautiful cover designs on both the soft cover and hard cover editions of this book.

To Louise Hay for pioneering the body/mind/spirit movement long before it was socially acceptable. I have studied your work since 1987 and am honored that I was able to express my gratitude to you personally a few months ago.

To Hay House's Reid Tracy, in the last couple of years you have guided me in the following workshops: *Write, Speak and Promote; Write From My Soul;* and various *Writer's Workshops.* I've had multiple opportunities to call in and ask you specific questions; thank you for all of the amazing content you and your incredible team at Hay House have shared.

To Cheryl Richardson for teaching me the concept of self-care. Your book *The Art of Extreme Self-Care* changed my life.

To Karen Drucker and John Hoy for the use of your song *What One Woman Can Be* as the theme song for my business (and my life).

To Steve Sisgold, thank you for sharing your wisdom and insight. Working with you helped me to embrace my gifts and talents and to become willing to share them with the world.

To Christine Kloser and the Transformational Author Group, thank you for the love and support as I've trudged this path.

To Dr. Joe Dispenza and the Encephalon staff, who have taught me how to shift/develop many of my spiritual beliefs. Dr. Joe, I will always be grateful for your mind-blowing ability of taking both spiritual and scientific concepts and putting them into ordinary, everyday language.

To Barry Goldstein for your remarkable music. Each time I've been able to sing/dance your song *Om, Shalom,*

Home in your presence, my heart has opened deeper than before.

To Dr. Lissa Rankin, my energetic and spiritual role model the last few years. Lissa partnered with the following incredible souls: Amy Ahlers, Bruce Cryer, Melanie Bates and Beth Elliott to create the Visionary Ignition Mastermind group.

To the spirit-minded members of Visionary Ignition Mastermind group who have each had a tremendous impact on my life. Amy Marsh Draper, Christina Haas, Sheryl Samuels Greenfield, Tammy Johns Pittenger, Erin Mitchell, Measha Peterson Dancy, Kim Marshall, Christy Clay, Salley Sedgwick, Julie Horsley, Allie Stark, and Kim Roberts; thank you for your fabulous support.

To Jamie Marich for creating *Dancing Mindfulness* and convincing me ANYBODY can dance. I am very proud of being a certified *Dancing Mindfulness* facilitator, because they are words I never thought I would use to describe myself.

To my Book Shaman-Editor Melanie Bates, the final drafts of this manuscript could not have been completed without your ability to see and hear me and my story. You have touched my heart and soul in more ways than I can put into words. I will be forever grateful.

To Di Larson, although you considered your editing contribution "small," I remain humbled by and grateful for your review, thank you!

To Linda Sprigg, your consistent friendship over the years has meant the world to me. Thank you for reviewing my manuscript and helping me find my lost 'to's. You have had a front row seat to my journey and I am honored and grateful to call you my friend.

To Alan Kaufman for your legal advice and editing. You have raised my confidence in my ability to tell the truth about my story.

To Sharyl Vope for swooping in at the last minute and providing the finishing touches on my manuscript. Proving once again, our SoulTen truly does stand together and have each other's back. I appreciate your brilliance and the beauty of your spirit.

To my marketing teams at *Stern: A Nationwide Website Design and Online Marketing Agency*; *Global Visibility*; *Expert Insights Publishing*; *Powerteam International* and *Balboa Press Publishing* thanks for everything you have contributed to my business and helping me get my story out in the world.

To all of my friends and family whom I have not mentioned personally, thank you for the roles you have played in my life. I look forward to seeing what our futures hold. I truly do love each of you.

Printed in the United States
By Bookmasters